Testimonies from God's Servants

A Compilation of Missionary Stories

JUNE BARRON

Testimonies from God's Servants
A Compilation of Missionary Stories

June Barron
Copyright © 2021 J Barron Ministries
Published by Inkhorn Writers
info@inkhornwriters.com

All rights reserved. No part of this book may be translated or reproduced without the written permission of the copyright owner.

Unless otherwise indicated, all scripture references in this book are taken from the New King James Version of the Bible, copyright © 1982 by Thomas Nelson Inc., Nashville, Tennessee.

Scripture quotations marked KJV are taken from the King James Version, Public domain. Scripture quotations marked ESV are taken from the ESV® Bible (The Holy Bible, English Standard Version®), copyright © 2001 by Crossway, a publishing ministry of Good News Publishers. Used by permission. All rights reserved. Scripture quotations marked CEV are taken from the Contemporary English Version © 1991, 1992, 1995 by American Bible Society. Used by permission. Scripture quotations marked NIV are taken from the Holy Bible, NEW INTERNATIONAL VERSION®, NIV® Copyright © 1973, 1978, 1984, 2011 by Biblica, Inc.® Used by permission. All rights reserved worldwide.

ISBN: 9798532238299

Table of Contents

Introduction 1
Chapter One: Marina Adams 4
Chapter Two: Malcolm Alcock 26
Chapter Three: Gladys Coutinho 39
Chapter Four: Margo Doody 41
Chapter Five: Brian and Jen Friend 56
Chapter Six: Deborah Gaffney 59
Chapter Seven: Premdan Majhi 66
Chapter Eight: Thelma Pallas 72
Chapter Nine: Richard John Perry 75
Chapter Ten: Barbara Pollard 80
Chapter Eleven: Elaine Price 93
Chapter Twelve: Keith Wilson 103
Chapter Thirteen: Gill Witton 111
Photographs 116

Acknowledgements

Above all else we first give glory to the Lord, who inspired dear souls to venture to the mission-fields of the world with whatever time and resources they were able to give. Some became short term mission folk, delivering help to those permanently based in the field, and some went on to become full-time missionaries themselves.

This book gives a brief glimpse at several varied folks who obeyed the call. They are unsung heroes, like the little ships at Dunkirk – going, giving, sending and working with the persecuted and trafficked, and encouraging in whatever way they could. You will find that they are ordinary folk with an amazing reputation for obedience to God.

In the midst of these folks' stories, you will read how some of them ministered with, to, and alongside pastors and ministries in persecuted regions. For the safety of the pastors and ministries, we have abbreviated their names for their protection and the protection of their flocks.

I would like to thank Mr. Ashley Treacy for all of his hard work and patience. Ashley studied all the handwritten stories, and then typed them out. His contribution was invaluable.

I hereby acknowledge the brave souls who overcame their modesty to write a portion of their own adventures, in order to encourage others to do the same. Each one of them could write a full book of their own if they became so inspired. Because this book is, as it were, a sampler, sadly some stories were unable to be fitted in, but we are encouraging those prolific writers to embark on their own books. May the sample portions in this book inspire them and others to launch into whatever ministry the Lord has next for them.

I want to thank the spouses and children, family members and all supporters who enabled the short termers to go and sow and grow.

I want to thank Pastor Debbie Dailey for pulling this book into being a book, and I pray that God will be glorified in it all.

I encourage each of you to picture yourself in each story and to remember your own stories as you read this book.

God bless you.

June <><

About the Writers

Let me briefly introduce you to what I know of the varied experience of our writers, and what I perceive their many adventures have involved, with apologies if I have missed some vital truth.

Mrs Marina Adams – Republic of Ireland and Northern Ireland
> Marina is a gracious saintly woman of prayer who is active in Northeast India with mission building, baby rescue and ministering.

Mr Malcolm Alcock – England and Isle of Man
> Malcolm is a cheery friendly saint and prayer warrior who is active in Chernobyl, India and Africa with building projects and ministering.

Mrs Gladys Coutinho – India and Scotland
> Gladys is a mighty woman of prayer who is active in Northeast India with medical camps and ministering.

Miss Margo Doody – Republic of Ireland
> Margo is a lover of Jesus and prayer who is active in Israel, India and Ireland with prayer and support.

Mr & Mrs Brian and Jen Friend – England, U.K. and Africa
> Brian and Jen are mature, respected and fruitful Christian leaders who are active in many spheres of influence with projects and ministering.

Mrs Deborah Gaffney – England and Scotland
> Deborah is a lover of Israel who is active with feeding programs for Holocaust survivors.

Mr Premdan Majhi – India and Northern Ireland
  Premdan is active in Northern Ireland and in the India tea gardens ministering.

Mrs Thelma Pallas – England
  Thelma is active in England faithfully exhorting the church with lockdown letters.

Mr Richard Perry – England and Scotland
  Richard is active in Scotland, Eastern Europe and India supporting ministries and passionately ministering.

Mrs Barbara Pollard – England
  Barbara is effective in prayer and active in England and Northeast India with ladies and children's ministry, and evangelism.

Mrs Elaine Price – Wales
  Elaine is a prayer leader who is active in Northeast India touring Welsh revival locations and ministering about Israel.

Mr Keith Wilson – England
  Keith is a prayer warrior who is active in Northwest and Northeast India supporting and ministering.

Gill Witton – England and Wales
  Gill is active in Northeast India ministering and as a co-prayer leader with Elaine Price.

Introduction
June Barron, England, UK

My name is June Barron. At this moment in time, I am writing some of my memoirs and watching God build His mission in India, just as He said He would.

In 2007 I stood on twenty-seven acres of beautiful land that had been given for free in 2005 that would fulfil a mission vision given me by the Lord several years earlier. For the umpteenth time I was requesting visiting guests to pray for the mission vision I had seen. We had three guests with us in India right then: one English woman and a husband-and-wife from Ireland. The English guest left us to position herself in the area where the orphanage and administrative centre was to be built, and there in that earthquake zone she prayed. Within two years of supernatural provision and work, we were dedicating the completed unshakeable building complex she had prayed for. Her name is Barbara Pollard.

Whilst Barbara was praying alone, I walked pretty much to the centre of the thick jungle-like land with the husband-and-wife guests. To my surprise they did not pray with us all so we would be in a prayer of agreement, but they separated from us and began to intercede. As they did this, I had a terrifying sensation of the presence of our Holy God. His presence was convicting me of the nearness of a hell I deserved. I was, until then, unaware of my current standing when the Lord began showing me that I had a resentment and unforgiveness dominating me. As the Lord revealed my dangerous position, I was helpless. I realized what He had shown me was true, but I didn't know how to put it right. There on the virgin jungle land I begged Him to help me put right what seemed impossible for me to do and trusted Him to help me to do it.

I remembered why we were on the land, and so I silently prayed a very personal honest prayer. The vision the Lord had shown me in September of 1998 was of a mission to be built in India. I had spent seven years searching for the location and travelled to over fourteen different states with many saints joining in from time to time. During those years I had gathered many ministry contacts. Now, exactly as He had told me it would happen, He gave me the land to build His mission and the people group of His choice to build it. Upon the giving of the land the other searchers rejoiced, but I cringed in terror! How was I supposed to build this mission? Now, standing on the land, repentant and humble, I copied the prayer of the father who was seeking help for his son. I asked for the faith to do my part in building what He had shown me, and I knew I was nowhere near such a qualification. So, I said, "Lord I believe, help thou my unbelief!" He told me to get on my knees, and I did. There on the jungle floor nearby to wild elephant dung, I waited for His instruction. He told me to come on my knees daily and look at this place, that I would see that He is doing it, and to give Him the glory. He continued to tell me that He Himself would build His mission, and I would give Him the glory. He was extremely stern in the telling, and I would not forget such an encounter. Six months later, three beautiful Indian saints prayed a blessing on me (unknowingly covering that area of resentment and unforgiveness), and God's grace intervened, and the matter was healed.

That was in 2007. Today here I am still daily going on my knees and looking at the place, still repeating that He is building His mission and that I will give Him all the glory.

I am unsure that it is entirely fair to only give God the glory for building His mission and not also give Him the glory for all of His grace towards me and others. So, I asked His permission to also give testimony of other parts of my life, and I asked for His help to do it.

I have spent some time convincing others to begin writing their testimonies, too. Many were already feeling the unction to do this, even if only for their family members. So, in this book you will read only the tip of their icebergs.

I pray that somehow through the small contributions in this book that we all will show how great our God is, for He deserves all the glory. Amen!

Chapter One: Marina Adams
Northern Ireland, UK

Life's Journey

A few friends have been saying to me that I should write my experiences down. I am not very good at keeping records so what I share here are some of the memories that have stayed with me. As I reflect on life, it seems much like a train journey with its stations, route changes and accidents. At birth we board the train and meet our parents, who we believe will always travel by our side. However, at some station our parents will step down from the train, leaving us to journey alone. As time goes by, other people who will be significant board the train – siblings, friends, children and the love of our life. Many people will step down throughout the journey and leave a permanent vacuum, while others who step down will go unnoticed. The journey will be full of joy, sorrow, fantasy, expectation, hellos, goodbyes and farewells. Success in the journey consists of having a good relationship with all the passengers and requires that we give the best of ourselves. The mystery is that we do not know at which station we ourselves will step down, so we must live in love and forgiveness and offer the best of who we are. It is important to do this because when the time comes for us to step down and leave our seat empty, we should leave behind beautiful memories for those who continue to travel on the train of life. As I look back over my years and the different events that have taken place, I see them as arriving at different stations in my life.

Chapter One: Marina Adams

I first boarded the train in September 1943 with my parents George and Frances Magahy. I was the second child; my brother was two years older than me. We lived on a small farm outside a town called Shercock in County Cavan, Republic of Ireland. My father was a blacksmith and owned a forge in the town. All the farmers used to come to get new shoes on their horses ("shod", as they called it). He did other things too, like welding. My mother stayed at home and looked after the farm. She kept some livestock to earn extra money to educate us two children. Our primary school was an ordinary house with one classroom, one teacher and fifteen pupils. The church and the graveyard were on the grounds behind the school, which left the graveyard as our playground. Every Sunday we attended the church, at which my father was the caretaker. My brother and I had to go in every Saturday to dust the pews and gather firewood to light the stove for the Sunday morning service. The pews were lovely shiny brown wood. I remember my brother in his short trousers sliding along the pew to speed up the dusting process. My brother progressed steadily through school and to Kings College Hospital, a boarding school in Dublin. I don't think he was so happy there as apparently there was no nonsense in those days and the prefects were hard on him (the belt was used on many occasions and probably much of it deserved).

One particular day, when I was nine years old and still in primary school, I remember my father going off to work. It was a county-fair day in the town and children didn't go to school on a fair day, which turned out to be a blessing on this occasion. I was still in bed when I heard my mother call out. I went up to her bedroom to find she had a severe pain in her chest and noticed her colour changing. I thought she had fainted because I used to faint at school, especially when the doctor came to vaccinate us or when the dentist would visit to inspect our teeth.

Believe me the doctor and the dentist didn't have any pity on us (all I had to do was look at them and I would faint) so I thought my mother had fainted. I tried to give her a drink of water with no success, so I ran down the lane to a neighbour, but she wasn't at home. Her brother told me she had gone down to the main road to wait for a man who was coming to pick up turkeys she had for sale. I rushed down to the road to get her. After waiting on the man to buy the turkeys, we eventually made it back up to the house but by this time mum had passed away. I always remember our dog Sheila, a beautiful black Labrador, crying so hard outside in the yard (how animals can be so sensitive). That was my first station for a change of direction – it was a hard platform.

Over the next few years after leaving primary school, I lived with three different families (one cousin and two different aunts). I remember on one occasion when the aunt I was living with was talking to her minister and they were discussing sending me to Doctor Barnardo's children's' home in Belfast. Thankfully, my father intervened and put an end to that situation. After that, I spent some time with her son and his family who lived in Dublin. However, one day I got a phone call from my other aunt's husband (my uncle) who lived in Lisburn, where we used to spend family holidays.

My uncle gave me instructions to get on the train in Dublin the following day and get off at Lisburn, where he would meet me. He said my fare was paid for, so off I went. This would be a new beginning for me as my train journey had just taken a different direction. This aunt and uncle had two girls, and we had much fun together. I felt a sense of security with them and felt that I was part of their family. I was fifteen years of age at this stage, and it was decided I should do nursing. I was too young to go into training, so I got a job at Clifton House in Belfast as a probationer nurse (as they called it in those days). Clifton House was a large ancient building that was renovated from a workhouse to a nursing home. The matron there was very nice and good to all her staff. The pay was poor, but I got my keep and food, which was a bonus. It was also a place to get a good grounding before starting a career in nursing.

When I reached eighteen, I applied to do a three-year course to train as a state registered nurse (SRN) in Lurgan Hospital. During that year my father, who was in his fifties, passed away. After finishing my general training, I went to Bellshill, Scotland outside of Glasgow to do midwifery training with two wonderful friends, Joan and Breidge. The three of us had a wonderful time in Scotland. When we returned from Scotland each of us got posts in the maternity unit in Lurgan Hospital and lived with Joan's parents. Her parents were wonderful to us, and I will never forget their kindness and the wonderful laughter we had. Joan's mum was a character. Joan and I had the privilege of holding her hand as she went home to be with the Lord in 2013 at the age of ninety-eighth. That was a sad year for Joan as she had also lost her husband earlier in the year. Joan still lives close by and has always been there for me. She and I still keep our friendship open with Breidge, and we meet up on occasion.

My brother eventually emigrated to Canada where he had a good job, married an Irish girl and became well settled. They came over for a holiday shortly after the wedding and invited me to go to Canada. I said that I would think about it, and I did. I thought to myself, I am a free agent with no responsibilities, why not! Leaving my best friends would be hard, however, two other colleagues thought it would be a good idea for them to try Canada as well. So, I was the one to go first and pave the way, as it were.

In the summer of 1967, my two best friends and Joan's mum (to keep us on the right track) dropped me off at Dublin Airport where I boarded a big Aer Lingus plane that was headed to Toronto, Canada. While boarding, I looked down the aisle of the plane and it appeared as though it had no end. I got to my seat, settled in, and then noticed that the sound system was playing lovely relaxing music. Suddenly, the music changed and the song "I'll Take You Home Again Kathleen" began to play, which activated the tears.

It took me some time to settle in Canada. I got a job in a nearby hospital and was very happy there. I was living in an apartment with a couple of Canadian girls, so I had to get used to pizza and pasta, which was something that hadn't been introduced to Ireland as yet.

The year following my arrival in Canada, my train journey took a different direction – I met the love of my life, an Irishman named Tommy. We met in February of that year and our relationship quickly flourished to marriage in October (no long engagement). The couple Tommy was staying with at the time said we would last six months, but thankfully fifty-two years later we have travelled a good and long journey together. Of course, there were highs and also lows (and blows), but we pushed through them together.

We settled in a small town called Newmarket, around fifty miles north of Toronto and were the proud owners of a lovely bungalow. In 1970 we had a beautiful daughter, Sandra, who was and is the apple of our eye. She is now married with two lovely boys who are growing quickly into young adults.

Tommy and I had very busy lives in Canada. I was working

Chapter One: Marina Adams

full time in York County Hospital in Newmarket and Tommy was working in Toronto doing shift work. We were like ships passing in the night. Tommy probably had itchy feet and really wasn't very happy in his job, and leaving Sandra with a babyminder was hard. In the wintertime, coming home from work at midnight and having to get a shovel out to clear the driveway of snow in order to park the car was not good. One day Tommy brought the subject up about returning home to Ireland. I loved Canada and the hospital and had made many friends, so I really wasn't that keen on returning to Ireland. However, I gave in (as you do) and we made plans to return home.

We packed up eventually and decided to travel home on a ship instead of going by air as we had a motor home that we decided to bring back with us. We had a couple stormy nights on board, but apart from that it was very nice, and we met a Canadian man, whose father was a Baptist pastor. He was going to Ireland to get married to a girl from Falls Road in Belfast. When the ship docked, we were able to give him a lift from Southampton to the ferry across to Dublin, where we left him to make his way to Belfast.

Tommy and I eventually reached Cavan at my in-law's house. I had already met my in-laws on one of our trips back home after we were married. They were lovely country folk, nothing complicated about them, and we had a great relationship. They accepted me into the family as if I was one of their own, and I had the privilege of praying with both of them in their latter days with the assurance of heaven.

At this point, the train journey was on another line. Tommy and I decided to move to Northern Ireland. My friend Joan and her husband Jim were kind enough to shelter us until we bought a house. After a couple of moves we ended up in Enniscrone Park. We decided to have another child, and in December 1976 our son Keith was born. We now had our boy and girl. Keith is now married and has two lovely children named India and Daniel. India got her name because she was conceived in India when both parents were on a mission trip where Keith preached the Gospel. The Lord used them both and they saw the hand of God at work. I continue to travail in prayer to see Keith take up the call, and I will not give up. I had a part time job at the Craigavon Area Hospital, which was good as I was able to look after our children myself. I attended the local Church of Ireland occasionally but had no real desire to get involved, however, one morning an envelope came through my letterbox and inside was an invitation to study the gospel of John. It was a weekly study that was done through the post. Every week I got instructions on what to read and I had to answer questions. It was very easy, nothing difficult or complicated about it until it came to the last letter that asked the question, "Where was I in the centre of God's life?" That was a question I couldn't answer, so that was the end of the study, although it didn't stop me thinking about the question.

I made friends with my neighbour next door, Hilary, and she introduced me to a Methodist church. I found it to be a very friendly place, so I started to go there on a regular basis. Sometime later, a missionary named Reverend Jack Craigmile came to speak in the church. God had been nudging Tommy and me to Him for some time and one evening at the mission meeting both of us were very brave and gave our lives to the Lord Jesus. We were both delighted with our newfound faith, and we had each other for encouragement.

Time passed and both Tommy and I were well settled back

in Ireland. It was always our desire to build a house in the country, so we spent a lot of time driving around the countryside trying to find a plot for sale to build on. Finally, our dream came true, and we found a place that was perfect. It was an old cottage with a tin roof and plenty of sheds in the yard, perfect to knock down and build a new house and a big garage for Tommy. Eventually, we started to build. We used to come out every evening to view the progress and see how the builder was getting on and would carry bricks up the ladder to give a helping hand. On one occasion, Tommy arrived and there was Will, the builder, on one knee with his cap over the other knee praying over the foundation. I always remember that image when I see how God has used our home and how we made contact with so many different Christians from all over the world. It has been a joy.

We finally moved into our newly built home. After living in a makeshift room with only a shower, it was a luxury to get a long soak in a bath. However, this is where the journey took on another route. I discovered a lump on my breast, which turned out to be malignant. It was a very traumatic time for us all as a family. I needed surgery and I had much to think about. I had seen a notice in a window uptown that there was a healing service in the home of John Greenaway. I had a great desire to attend it. Next thing I knew my friend Joan arrived to see me with the same healing meeting notice in her hand that she had cut out of a newspaper. It was confirmation for me that I had to go but there was just one problem – the meeting was on the evening before I had to go to the hospital for a total mastectomy. There was much prayer and hoping that all preparations were complete and that I would get permission to be allowed out that evening. Tommy and Jim (Joan's husband) had done a trial run to make sure we wouldn't get lost in the countryside. My prayer was answered, and I got permission from the surgeon. The doctor more or less gave me the impression that he believed I was going out to drown my sorrows. I steadfastly went to the meeting where I received prayer, and after which I knew all would be well and that I was healed. When I arrived at the hospital the next day, they gave me a sleeping pill that ended up in the bin as I was too excited to go to sleep. Next morning a nurse came in who obviously knew something was going on because she told me that I was not going through with the surgery. She was spot on. The surgeon came to talk to me, and we agreed that I would come back in a week.

That week in my life was one that I will never forget. I felt the Lord's presence so strong, and I knew that all was well. I knew it was a week given to me to prepare myself for when I went back. I went through surgery the following Thursday without any problems, followed by five weeks of radiotherapy. I give God all the glory for His healing. Thirty-three years later, it is something I rarely ever think of.

My next train journey made a big impact in my life. I got to know this wonderful lady named Dorothy who lived in Laurelvale. Dorothy was a lady that seemed to have the right answer to every problem. She used to have meetings in her home, and it was through those meetings that I met two ladies who came over from England on occasions to the meetings. One lady was Betsy, who was a converted ex-nun, and the other was Jean. These two ladies worked together in the gifts of the Holy Spirit, and I got to know the ladies very well. After they prayed with me, something changed within me. As I was reading my Bible I was noticing things that I had never seen before. The Bible opened up to me in a different and new way as I began seeing things in a new light. Sometime later Betsy and Jean were having meetings in our home and Dorothy arranged to have a water baptism in our back garden. We filled up a fairly big children's pool with water, which was great. The only setback was that it poured down rain but that didn't matter since we were soaked anyway, and the joy of the Lord was our strength. It was glorious to see many young people come to the gathering to be encouraged and filled with the Holy Spirit. I brought Jean and Betsy to different homes where people requested prayer. Sadly, a few months later Dorothy developed cancer. She came to stay with me for a week during her illness and we spent lovely moments together that I will always cherish. Many were heartbroken over her death. And then, sadly, Jean passed away a few years later.

Through Dorothy's ministry, I came to know another Christian lady from England named Reverend June Barron (known in India as Mama June). At one of her visits, she was due to go back home the next morning but needed someone to bring her to the airport, for which I volunteered. The next morning, I picked her up and I told her that if she was ever looking for a lift, not to hesitate to call me since I was retired and it was no problem. She responded that she had just prayed for somebody to come on board as circumstances had changed with the person who previously was able to help her. At that moment, a new relationship started with June and myself, and I knew it was God.

Commissioned to India

A different journey would begin with this new relationship, one that was unexpected. June had been to India on missionary trips many times, usually a couple of times a year preaching in different areas, mostly in Northeast India in the province of Meghalaya. She had a vision from God to build a mission centre that had an orphanage, educational school, trade school, clinic, and training workshops. The vision also included agricultural land for food, playgrounds, gardens for orchards and a circular auditorium for spiritual teaching. The mission centre would have Christian caretakers to help heal the wounded and oppressed. It would be built by those who loved God and wanted to be a part of what He wants done because God loves His little children, no matter what age they have reached.

As we had become friends, June invited me to go on a trip to India, which was something I never would have thought about ever happening. Imagine me going to India! However, I got my India visa and necessary jabs and was ready to go. There were a couple of other folks who had their own fellowship churches and other Christians going so we all met up and travelled together. My first encounter with India was landing in the Calcutta airport. There weren't many people about except for a very thin pregnant cat watching everybody come through the airport. The heat was in the 30°C range, and my glasses started to steam up after getting off the flight into the dense heat. We then had to get a taxi to bring us to a hotel where we stayed overnight. We had two men with us, Colin and Garry, who took control, kept us in order and looked after us. One of the lady's cases didn't arrive so she was left only with what was on her back. It was a few days before her case arrived, however, I had some extra necessities that came in handy. India opened up a new world to me and is a story to tell on its own.

My trips to India have touched my heart in many ways as I travelled to different villages with Mama June and other ministries. We saw many people give their lives to Jesus and saw many healed from different conditions. Like everywhere else in the world there is sickness that comes in many different forms (physical, spiritual, emotional, et cetera). Many people had family problems, so their hearts were very open to the gospel and to the belief that God would heal them, and He does. Many of the people work in the rice paddy fields and they don't have the money to visit a doctor. Quite often they must simply believe that they will be healed, and many do get healed instantly.

I would have a problem sharing everything that happened in India, so I will give you some of the experiences that are forever etched on my heart. On one occasion, we drove many miles on a very rough path to do a medical camp. A pastor's wife who was with us was very experienced with medical camp ministry. She knew all the medications and what they were for, and her being able to speak the language was a great advantage. There were many parents with children who had high temperatures, as malaria was a big problem. It was a different side of district nursing than I was used to.

There was a lady who lived in a little hut close by the medical camp. All she owned was a small pot that she had in the middle of the floor and a stool to sit on. She showed me her bedroom, which had a bed but no mattress or blanket. We were able to give her a warm blanket for which she was very appreciative.

The daughter of Doctor C (a local doctor and pastor) brought me to see a lady who lived in a little hut across the hills from her home. The lady depended on a nearby family to help her and to give her food. I gave her some rupees to sustain her, and honestly, I will never forget looking at the joy on her face. I was told later she was going around dancing, singing and praising God that He had answered her prayer and that she could buy a jar of Ovaltine – such joy over a jar of Ovaltine. Memories like this are simple yet mean so much. I just want to give thanks to our heavenly Father for all His provision.

On another occasion, after visiting a village with Pastor J (a local pastor) we were on our way home down a very narrow road in a jeep when we came upon an area where a Hindu festival was taking place. A bus had broken down on the road, which meant we couldn't get past and go any further. It was scary as we found ourselves in the middle of a Hindu festival with all the people bringing animals for sacrifice. There were three of us with very white faces in the jeep: Jean from Ireland (who had lovely silver hair), Leigh from Ireland and of course me. We were parked beside a big field that was filled with goats and hens and had two spotlights beaming across it. I was beginning to become fearful for all of us as I watched what was going on, however, the bus finally moved onto the side of the road, and we were able to move on. Pastor J said that field would be soaked in blood in the morning from the slaughter of animals. I give thanks to Jesus that He became our sacrifice and that we don't need to sacrifice animals.

On another outing, Pastor J had promised to call on a pastoral friend as we were returning home from a village. When we arrived at the village, his whole congregation was there to greet us. Word must have been spread that white people were calling. Some of the folks had never seen a white person and wanted to touch our skin and listen to us talk. As visitors, we were asked to give a little talk about ourselves or whatever we wanted to share. I was learning, or trying to learn, how to say hello in Garo. I made an attempt to say hello, and I was quite pleased with myself thinking I had the pronunciation right, but I wondered why everyone was laughing. Apparently, what I had said was, "Do you want a good slap?" I still get reminded about the mishap by certain people.

Another lovely memory of India was a safari trip. June had

assigned me to go with Pastor Cáit on her visits to different churches in the Garo Hills. Pastor Cáit is from Carlow, Ireland where she has a fellowship called God's House of Prayer for all Nations. We had a lot of fun time together as we had stayed overnight in many different places. There was a lot of ministry and many people needing prayer. We had a very busy week so one day Pastor J decided to take us on a safari and picnic prepared by some of the ladies from the church. We set off with Pastor J, his niece and nephew up a narrow path in a jeep. We came to an office where we had to sign in and could have a comfort stop, which was a hole in the ground. We continued our journey and the further we went along this narrow road it was like you were driving on top of the jungle, over the trees. To look down the side of the path was very scary and if you went off track and fell down the side it would be goodbye. On a couple of occasions, we had to stop and remove logs that wild elephants had put across the path because they don't like intruders. As we journeyed on our way, we came across a bird sitting in the middle of the road, and it made no attempt to move. Pastor J jumped out and lifted the bird and brought it into the jeep. The bird didn't try to get away nor was it concerned that it might be in any danger. Pastor J said it was an Emerald Dove; its name just fitted so well. It had the most beautiful emerald-green wings that just shimmered in the sunshine. We were so amazed at this beautiful bird. It was a great topic of conversation. Pastor Cáit mentioned that Ireland is called the Emerald Isle. I then noticed the bird's orange beak and said that Cáit is from green south Ireland, and I am from orange north Ireland. We had a good laugh! Pastor J's niece was holding the bird and discovered the bird had only one leg, which led to a prophetic revelation of the orange North and green South division in Ireland. When we got to the end of the road we gave the bird a drink from the cap of a bottle of water, and you could see its countenance change as it drank. When we met up with the folks from the church, we all got into a circle and prayed for Ireland. While we prayed, the bird was sitting on a big leaf and didn't move, and then a white circle appeared above us. When we finished praying the bird spread his beautiful wings and flew off, across the jungle. What an experience. Only God could do something like that. After all the excitement we had a lovely picnic of rice mixed with finely chopped veg wrapped in a big leaf. Where we were parked it looked as if we were on top of the jungle, looking over it. On our drive home we came across three elephants that looked like mum, dad and baby. After admiring them for a few minutes the father elephant gave a roar as though telling us that we had seen enough, keep moving. What a wonderful encounter, that in the midst of a jungle God shows up and blesses us. It was a beautiful experience that will always stay with me.

My next memorable moment is of the day we travelled quite a distance for a meeting. After we parked the jeep, we had to walk quite a way on a rough path to a beautiful field with a ravine flowing alongside. There was a lovely breeze and the sound of the trees rustling in the wind. It reminded me of the beautiful song "I Hear the Sound of Rustling in the Leaves of the Trees" (by Ronnie Wilson).

> The Spirit of the Lord has come down on the earth.
> The church that seemed in slumber has now risen from its knees,
> And dry bones are responding with the fruits of New birth.
> Oh this is a time for declaration.
> The word will go to all men everywhere.

> The church is here for the healing of the nations.
> Behold the day of Jesus drawing near.
> My tongue will be the pen of a ready writer;
> And what the Father gives me I will sing,
> I only want to be His breath,
> I only want to Glorify the King.

The beautiful field and ravine, and sound of the trees rustling in the wind is a scene forever etched on my heart. Oh, that the Spirit would come down on the earth for such a time as this and the church rise from its knees. How God is being taken out of so much in society and sin is being embraced, targeting our children and indoctrinating them by sinful ideas. Thank God for godly parents who tell their children the truth.

There were people coming from everywhere for the meeting in that beautiful field. No matter how far you travel in India, there are always people about. They just seem to come out of every hole in the hedges. Pastor Cáit was there, and two Indian pastors. Pastor Cáit gave the message, and then it was time for prayer ministry. I was given an interpreter and put in a line to pray for people and minister. Coming from my church in Northern Ireland, prayer lines were something we did not practise; it was always the pastors who did the praying for people. However, *must do* is a great innovator, and thankfully God showed up once more – He is faithful in every way! A lovely tall man came for prayer. I seemed so small standing beside him, and I can still see his lovely polished brown shoes. The interpreter spoke to him, and she then turned to me and said, "He is blind". I turned around to look for one of the pastors, saying to myself, "Oh, this is too much for me". But the pastors were all busy praying with people, so I said within myself to the Lord, "Lord you made the blind to see when You were here on earth, so I'm asking You now to heal this blind man in the name of Jesus". The interpreter and the man started talking, and I could see him blinking and rubbing his eyes since the sun was shining, and the brightness had hit him. She said, "He can see!". Wow! What a miracle! Our God is a God of miracles. What jubilation! That was a big faith booster!

Another memorable moment is one of meeting a young man with YWAM named Abhi who worked with the children of the sex workers in the red-light district of Mumbai. Abhi invited June, two young Irishmen, husband-and-wife pastors and me to visit him in Mumbai, to see the work he is doing. When we caught up with Abhi, he brought us to a building in the red-light district where he had a ministry room. The entryway into the building was long and lined with room after room, each having no door but only a curtain. Many of the sex workers were married and their husbands would take every rupee from them so that the women were left with no money and never had a chance to escape. I got a peep into one of the rooms, a place you would never want to be. We should never forget to thank God for what we have and how blessed we are, as we remember how many people around the world have to live in desperate situations. We made our way to a room that Abhi had for himself and where he had some toys and books for the children. He was great with the little ones, teaching them choruses and telling them Bible stories. He also had bought sewing machines for the ladies to make garments to sell to make extra money just for themselves. The madam who was in charge was friendly and greeted us. She looked as if she was getting on in years but had been a beautiful lady in her day. She had a little nine-month-old boy with her whose mother had died of aids. June told her that we could take the boy to our mission orphanage in the Garo Hills, but she was a bit hesitant until Abhi and a quite convincing talkative lady worker talked to her. After many discussions the madam gave her consent and we immediately began to make flight arrangements to Guwahati for her, the child and Abhi. All arrangements went well, and we met them at the Guwahati airport. Because Abhi knew the child, the boy was not scared. We set off for the six-hour drive over rough roads to the orphanage in the Garo Hills. I held the child on my knee minus a nappy, happily he slept the whole way with no accidents. Upon arrival at the orphanage, the child was prayed over by Pastor M, and he was renamed Peter. Peter settled in well with the other children and is still at the orphanage learning, growing and doing well.

The stories I have shared about my trips to India are just a small sample out of the many adventures I had there. In total, I have visited India five times, but now due to health problems it would be impossible for me to return. My husband and his friends have travelled to the orphanage twice to completely wire the first building and the extension, and to take the children on an overnight adventure to a zoo and water park. Great love exists forever between us all. We continue to watch the progress as our Indian friends get on with the job.

Destination Wales and Israel

My mission journeys have not stopped with India; they just changed to shorter flights and distances. One such mission was in June of 2018 when I met up with folks from America, India, Isle of Man, Northern Ireland, Southern Ireland, Wales, England and Scotland at a conference that June organized at the Bible College of Wales in Swansea. The Bible College of Wales is a lovely place. The grounds around it are magnificent, and it still carries the prayer anointing of Rees Howells, the founder of the college. We all gave a little nugget of testimony or teaching during the conference, which was very uplifting. There were also memorable days of visiting places where the Welsh Revival hit the hills of Wales, taking it over like a storm that became a hurricane. It was in 1904 that Evan Roberts travelled around Wales holding meetings. Society was deeply influenced by the renewed, law abiding individuals and their transformed personal lives that had become free of personal addictions. Thousands of people were saved, public houses became empty, men and women who used to waste their money getting drunk were now saving it and giving it to the church. Stealing and other offences were less and less, so much so that magistrates came to court and found no cases for them to try. Men who once continually blasphemed learned to talk purely, so purely that the pit ponies in the coal mines became disobedient because they were so used to be sworn at they didn't understand the pure talk. That is only a sample of how many lives were changed. It was so lovely to visit those chapels where Evan Roberts preached, like Pisgah Chapel. When you walk into Pisgah Chapel you cannot help but sense a powerful residual presence of God in the place. It's been 110 years since the revival, but God still watches over that hallowed place. Pisgah Chapel played a major role in the Welsh Revival, and it is now reopened as a prayer house for revival. My prayer is that it will be revived again and spread like a virus all over the world. Hallelujah!

Another journey that is so memorable was when I went to Israel where June introduced me to a Messianic Jew named Ariel. He was living in Jerusalem at the time but has since moved to Brazil. He is a wonderful Bible teacher and has travelled to many different countries teaching the word of God. He was fascinating to listen to and because of his Jewish background he brought the word to life in a different way. He was our tour guide in Israel. It was an amazing experience to walk where Jesus walked, to put my feet in the Sea of Galilee and to get into the Dead Sea (Salt Sea).

For Everything There is a Season

Life is moving on very quickly and I am very blessed. My husband is in good shape; however, I have had some health issues that have slowed me down. I underwent open heart surgery which was followed by some complications. It has taken time to recover but I know that I am not forsaken. My daughter Sandra and her husband Kyle have two lovely boys who we love very much. John is twenty-two years old as I write this and has completed a degree in theology, hoping to do a masters if everything falls into place. Peter is twenty years old, and he is doing a course in cybersecurity. They have both outgrown me at over six feet in height. Keith and Janice's daughter, India, is now eleven years old, and their son, Daniel, is nine years old. They are all wonderful and we love them.

As I look back, I thank God for how He has brought me from the little town that many people have never heard of to where I am today. I think back to my childhood of being a very shy child who when starting school wouldn't talk to anybody. My husband says I have certainly made up for it. I think of how I have travelled to Scotland, Canada, America, India, and Israel. Most importantly, I think of how God brought me to faith in Him. I thank God for how He has used our home for folks to stay in and to have meetings in, and how people's lives were changed. It reminds me of the builder who built our home and of the day Tommy saw him on one knee praying over the foundation. Because of the COVID-19 pandemic, I miss folks coming to our home and the fellowship we had together.

The world I knew growing up has changed so much, but I

thank God for His wonderful goodness to me over the years and His love for all of us. His grace is sufficient for every need. I just wouldn't be without Him in my life. No matter how we see things and no matter what is happening in our lives He is with us.

Ecclesiastes 3 sums life up in a wonderful way, "To everything there is a season, a time for every purpose under heaven". Solomon tells us God made a time for every purpose under heaven. There is the time of spring for the birth and development of your faith, and the time of summer for growth and maturity when you're becoming the person God desires you to be. There is fall in which you harvest the fruit of the things of which you have been developing all your life. And then there is winter. Wintertime can be a beautiful time, but it can also be a time of ending. For believers, winter leads to an eternal springtime in the presence of the Lord. There are also times in your life when things happen that you do not understand and cannot explain, and that no one else can explain or understand. There are things that can happen in the life of every believer from time to time for which you have no answer. It will happen. It happens in your health. It happens in your finances. It happens in your marriage. It happens in your business. It happens in your personal relationships with one another, and with people in your family. There are times in which you have racked your brain until it aches, and you cannot come up with an answer of why God is allowing something to happen. There are times when you are in a bitter Gethsemane – just you and the Lord – when your heart is broken, when life makes no sense, and when the frustration of your soul seems greater than your faith. In times of extreme adversity, this is the word from God that you must call to mind, "Your Father knows the things you have need of before you ask Him" (Matthew 6:8). It is not that chance has brought these things to you; it is in God's hand as it is meant to be – there is a time for every purpose under heaven.

As time moves on in this changing world, we don't know what tomorrow holds, but one thing we are sure of is the solid rock we have in Jesus Christ, all other ground is sifting sand. To the whosoever reading this reflection of my life may you be blessed in every way.

Chapter Two: Malcolm Alcock
England, UK

Be Careful What You Pray For

It was 1993 and God used Robert in answer to a prayer I made. Robert was now a committed believer, and he was changing for the better now that he had Jesus in his life. The Full Gospel Businessmen (FGB) were having another dinner meeting and the president of the fellowship had invited a man named Ivor. Ivor ministered to the poor and needy in Russia and the Ukraine. I invited Robert to come to the meeting as the guest speaker. As Ivor shared what God was doing in his ministry in Russia, I felt a longing in my heart to be involved somehow in that sort of ministry but wasn't sure how since I was financially challenged. I prayed saying, "Father, I would love to be able to do this type of ministry. Could you make this possible please? In Jesus' name". After the meeting ended, I felt led to introduce Robert to Ivor and they got to talking. By the end of their discussion, Ivor had invited Robert to come with him on his next trip to the Ukraine. Robert would be visiting Chernobyl, the site of one of the worst nuclear disasters in history. The Chernobyl disaster was a nuclear accident that occurred on Saturday, 26 April 1986 at the number four nuclear reactor in the Chernobyl Nuclear Power Plant near the city of Pripyat in North Ukraine.

A few weeks after the FGB meeting, Robert left with Ivor

to the Ukraine. When Robert returned, he promptly invited me to join him on the next trip, all to be paid for by Robert. Wow! I just stood amazed at how quickly God had answered my prayer, making true the scripture in Isaiah 65:24 that says, "And it shall come to pass, that before they call, I will answer and while they are yet speaking I will hear". That scripture was certainly for me, praise the Lord! And so started my journey as a wimpy missionary man!

Off to the Ukraine

Here I was at Heathrow Airport along with Robert, Ivor and Bernard about to board an Aeroflot aircraft that would take us to Kiev in the Ukraine. What an experience that flight was, and not one I want to repeat in a hurry. The flight was packed with mostly Russian or Ukrainian citizens returning home, and then us four British people. Ivor looked like a big hairy Russian, with his large beard and big-frame body. And there was Bernard who was a smaller person, friendly and full of Jesus. He was Ivor's right-hand man in the mission that Ivor had set up. Robert and I had never undertaken anything like what we were about to experience. Despite Robert's confident outlook, I suspected that he would have possibly been feeling like me – somewhat nervous, for sure. What was amazing about this flight was that when we landed everyone, and I mean everyone, clapped and cheered for the successful landing. Did that mean everyone knew something us British folks did not know? Was there always great anxiety and fear about an Aeroflot aircraft making a successful landing? I don't know, but I'm sure glad we were about the Lord's business and that He dispatched His angels around the aircraft to keep it from falling out of the sky or crash-landing.

After a nervous interrogation at immigration, we were all

allowed to collect our suitcases and go outside to meet our contact person that would take us to our accommodation at the home of the pastor who organized our program. Snow was falling quite hard as we set out on the road trip into the Kiev town centre. After a few hairy moments dodging oncoming traffic we arrived at our destination, which was a large block of flats where our host lived. Formalities were exchanged and we were then shown our sleeping quarters before tucking into a very Ukrainian meal, which was, to say the least, interesting! Our host was a very godly man, and his family couldn't do enough for us.

Our main focus for being in the Ukraine was to call on hospitals to see what they needed in the way of medical equipment. Our intention was to then ask our local hospital at home if they would donate items that were either out of date or they no longer had any need for. Our secondary focus was to see for ourselves the devastation caused by the Chernobyl nuclear accident. Our plan was to visit the site in order to get as much information as possible so that we could raise money to help the children who had been infected with the radiation leakage and to buy medical equipment for the nearby Ukrainian hospital.

With our focus on helping the children and providing hospital equipment, we only had time to attend one church meeting, which was held in the forest in a wooden hut accessed by rickety stairs. Bear in mind that openly holding religious meetings was still very much frowned on by the authorities, which is why the meeting took place in the forest. Before attending the meeting, I needed to go to the bathroom, which I obviously believed would be okay. Well, I soon found out that what I thought would be an okay toilet was in fact just a hole in the ground that seemed to attract every fly in the forest. When I noticed the flies dropping down dead from the smell, I knew that I was on 'mission impossible' to say the least! To survive the stench, I needed to hold my nose, which made going to the bathroom not easy – using one hand for the nose meant only having one hand free to attend to my toilet needs. Little did I know that this experience was actually preparing me (big time) for what I would later experience in future missionary travels for the Lord. Anyway, I was glad to successfully come away from the hole in the ground, not to mention I was glad that it was not a hole in the wall. After all the bathroom manoeuvring, I made my way into the meeting room.

The room was packed. I had never seen as much passion for Jesus as those Ukrainian believers demonstrated. Their prayers and their worship put me to shame. When they sang and prayed, they had tears in their eyes and cried out from their hearts. They really had true faith, and I began to think how dare I come here thinking that I had anything to give to these beautiful believers.

The meeting was led by Ivor, Bernard and Robert, with me just giving a brief testimony. After the meeting, I understood big time why my three colleagues had not been standing with me at the top of the stairs as the congregation were departing the meeting. I wondered why I was standing there on my own while those three stood a ways back, smiling. Well, I soon found out. You see, I am a people hugger by nature so when a person comes to me to say goodbye, I just hug them. They responded in kind, some of them being quite large, with overwhelming love. I will always remember those beautiful, genuine saints of God and their love and passion for Jesus that I sorely lacked.

Visiting the Hospital in Kiev

Visiting the top hospital in Kiev was an eye opener. We were shocked to see how deprived the hospital was of basic medical equipment. We witnessed a surgery where the patient had to bring his own bandages to cover his surgical wounds. In the UK, we don't realize how blessed and fortunate we are to have the wonderful National Health Service. All patients in the Ukraine have to pay for their surgery and medical care, and they have to supply their own bandages and the likes. After talking with the chief consultant of the hospital, we were able to get a comprehensive list of basic equipment and supply needs. We promised to try and get them what we could. In fact, when we went back on another trip, we were able to hand over a lot of medical equipment and supplies that were donated by various hospitals in the UK and the Isle of Man.

After spending time with the hospital chief, we visited some of the wards where children who had been victims of the radiation fallout at Chernobyl were being treated. We saw some horrific injuries and deformities that were the result of the radiation. I cannot bring myself to even write a description of what we saw. My heart bled for those souls who had not much life expectancy or any quality of life. Next, we were guided into a day-care room where we met with some thirty children along with their parents or caretakers. The four of us sang to them gospel songs and shared about Jesus and His love for them. Whilst we were singing, I noticed a young girl of five or six years of age in agony as she sat on her caretaker's lap. I felt the need for us to go and pray for her right there and then, so we gathered around her and prayed. Immediately she seemed free of the agony she had been in, and we later learnt that she was totally healed by God. Praise the Lord! After praying for the little girl, we were invited to pray for sick children in other wards. Seeing all the sick children had a profound effect on me. It gave me a deep passion to always pray for people to be saved, healed and set free from Satan's control in their lives. Lord, please allow me to be a channel for Your love to flow through and out of me to touch people's lives and draw them to You. I ask this in the name of Jesus Christ of Nazareth. Amen.

Chernobyl – A Silent Killer Released on the World

As most of you reading this will know, in April 1986 in northern Ukraine a nuclear meltdown of an atomic power plant caused a massive cloud of radiation to be emitted into the atmosphere killing many around the immediate vicinity. It also had a far-reaching impact on other countries. The radiation cloud even reached where I lived on the Isle of Man. On the highest hills of the Isle of Man, the farmers still cannot graze their sheep because of the contamination. The Chernobyl radiation core is still burning down into the ground there. Scientists from around the world have spent years trying to find a solution to contain the radiation and prevent further problems.

Robert, Ivor, Bernard and I were now driving from Kiev to Chernobyl, and we were not at all sure of what we were letting ourselves in for. We of course had prayed before commencing our journey and asked for God's protection and wisdom. We had to cross the border between Ukraine and Belarus to get to our destination, and as we approached the check point Bernard suddenly realised he had forgotten to bring his passport with him. We immediately prayed that God would blind the eyes of the guards so they wouldn't realize that they had not checked Bernard's passport and thus let us through. Well, the word of God says in Mark 11:24 "Therefore I say to you, whatever things you ask when you pray, believe that you receive them, and you will have them". Our prayers were answered, and we were allowed to proceed to our destination. Praise the Lord!

Because our visit to the Chernobyl nuclear site had to be

sanctioned by authorities, our guide had arranged permission to visit the site. He was told that someone would meet us five miles from the centre in order to transfer us from our car into a minibus that would take us to the site of the reactor. After duly transferring vehicles, and as we made our journey towards the nuclear reactor plant, we couldn't believe what we were seeing. Trees were stripped bare of their leaves, pinecones were deformed, and buildings had evidence of having been sprayed with bullets to force occupants to leave quickly. The silence was deafening; we could hear no birds singing and the mosquitos, flies and the like were big and strange looking. It definitely wasn't a place you would want to book as a holiday destination anytime soon.

We were driven to a large warehouse on the outskirts of Chernobyl where we were required to change our clothing. We had to put on boiler suits, along with what looked like a handkerchief to cover our heads and protective coverings over our shoes. We looked a sight to behold when we had a photo shoot later (not flattering, but worth it).

A Town Called Pripyat

We were driven to see the town called Pripyat where all the top scientists and their families who had worked at the nuclear plant had lived. The town was completely deserted. As we looked around, we noticed again that there were no birds singing and that everything was silent and eerie like a ghost town. We also noticed that the cement renderings on the buildings (which were mostly high-rise apartments) were crumbling and showing deformed structure bars, which we were told was the result of the radiation. Then (and this will always stick in my mind) we saw a large Ferris wheel (the type you see at fairgrounds) just standing there. The chairs that people would have sat in for their ride now moved slowly with the force of the wind, adding to the ghostly feeling of the place. But the worst was yet to come.

We were then taken to a graveyard of all the vehicles that were used to try and put out the fire at the reactor plant. Everyone who had been driving those trucks died or were severely affected by radiation poisoning. They were all the brave men and women who risked their lives to try and save many other people's lives. We were advised not to touch anything because there was still radiation in the metals on the vehicles. We were told that radiation can remain for over one thousand years.

The Chernobyl Research Centre

Our final destination was to meet the deputy director of the Chernobyl Research Centre. He was leading a team of top scientists from around the world who were still trying to find ways of capping damaged nuclear reactor number four with a massive concrete sarcophagus. The problem they faced was that the reactor site sat on marshy ground next to the river in Pripyat. The river flows into a major river course that flows into the Black Sea in South Ukraine. The Chernobyl Research Centre sits on land that had been completely stripped of all its soil and vegetation that had been contaminated by the radiation thus making the working environment safe for the scientists.

We asked the deputy director many questions, which he answered within the confines of his remit. One question that we asked was, "Is reactor number four still dangerous and are there other reactors in the Ukraine like this that caught fire?" His answer really shook us all. His reply was, "Yes, this reactor is still very dangerous because if the corium (a fuel-containing material or lava-like fuel created in the core of a nuclear reactor during a meltdown accident) burns down to the water table it will create an explosion seven times worse than that of the first explosion". He added that there were another three reactors on this site, plus another fifteen similar types of these reactors in and around the Ukraine. I recorded what he said on a dictaphone so that I would not forget it.

Once our meeting had ended with the deputy director we were taken back to the warehouse where we had changed our clothing coming in. Before leaving we had to be screened to see if there was any radiation on us from our visit but the Geiger counter they were using did not work. Do you remember the advert for Ready Brek Porridge where they showed a person with a glow around them that meant they were nice and warm from the porridge? Well, I am sure that we must have had a glow like that around us but not from porridge. I am so thankful for the assurances in Scripture, especially in Psalm 91:3 that says, "Surely He shall deliver you from the snare of the fowler and from the perilous pestilence". After putting back on our own clothes, we were driven back to our vehicle to return to Kiev.

In Kiev, we said our goodbyes to our host and returned home to the UK but not before one of our team nearly got arrested at the airport in the Ukraine because he had Ukrainian money on him, which was illegal to take out of the country. God again came to our rescue.

Of course, a lot more happened on this trip, but time and space doesn't permit to share all.

Sir Norman Wisdom and Our Return Trip to the Ukraine

Upon returning from our trip to Chernobyl, we set about raising funds and finding medical equipment for the hospitals in Kiev. We also were obtaining furniture for a respite centre that we were going to set up in Odessa near the Black Sea. This respite centre (which was a former army barracks) was to give children affected by the radiation of Chernobyl in that area the opportunity to go to Odessa to get fresh air and medical attention if needed.

To raise awareness for the need to help the Chernobyl victims, we were blessed to meet Sir Norman Wisdom, a very famous English comedian. We met him through our relationship with Rick Wakeman (the former keyboardist for the rock band Yes) and his wife Nina (a former beauty model). When Rick introduced us to Sir Norman, we shared our vision with him (although he isn't a Christian). He was so inspired he accepted an offer from us to become a patron of the charity that was to be set up to raise funds and highlight the awareness of the plight of the children. In fact, Sir Norman came on a visit to the Ukraine to see for himself what had happened. He was well loved and well received by all he met on the trip, and his involvement with the charity certainly helped to raise awareness.

After having secured medical equipment donated by various hospitals and the furniture for the respite centre, Robert, Bernard, Ivor and I loaded two large transit vans with everything. We then drove down to Dover where we would sail to Holland on a cargo boat. I made the foolish mistake of drinking the water from the tap in my cabin and I ended up having a severe bout of stomach issues. That was certainly a challenge to manage, especially whilst travelling through the countryside once we had left the boat.

We took four-hour turns driving the vehicles whilst the other person in the van slept behind the driver seat in a special sleeping-bunk. This worked out well because it meant we all rested properly and could travel nonstop to our various destinations. When we came to country borders, we had to show the custom officers what we had in each of the vans, in accordance with the manifest. At some border checkpoints, because we weren't giving the contents in the vans to that country, custom officers made it difficult for us by making us wait a long time to get clearance. Nevertheless, we counted it all joy when faced with these challenges, knowing that we were on a mission inspired by God to help people in need.

The saying "Be careful what you think as you might just get what you have thought" certainly came home to roost, big time for us because I foolishly thought a thought that instantly came to pass. So, what do I mean? Well, when we came to the border between East Germany and Poland, the custom official on the East Germany side promptly sealed the doors on the back of the vans after checking their contents. This meant we couldn't get into the back of the vans until the seals were broken by custom officers when we reached the border of Ukraine. One day, I was driving through beautiful but deserted forest areas in Poland with Robert sleeping. I was following Bernard and Ivor who were leading the way, when I suddenly thought, "What would happen if we were to have a puncture or a breakdown out in this deserted area? We wouldn't be able to get at our tools in the back of the vehicle because of the seal that the border guard put on our van doors". Well, as soon as I had this thought suddenly a large bang occurred and guess what? The back left-hand tyre of the leading van exploded causing the van to swerve side to side before Bernard, who was driving, managed to bring the van to a halt, narrowly missing a large ditch at the side of the road. Now what are we to do? We could not get access to our tools or spare tyre because of the seal on the back doors preventing access to the contents. But our God always sorts things out despite the actions of some of His children (well me of course, I was talking about here). God gave Bernard (a car mechanic by trade) the wisdom on how to break the seal without it looking like it had been broken. We managed to access the spare wheel and the tools but hit a problem because we needed to have the damaged tyre repaired. Leaving Robert and myself behind in our van, Ivor and Bernard went off in search of somewhere to fix the tyre. It was some three hours later before they came back, having successfully found somewhere to repair the tyre. Soon we were on our way through Poland heading towards Ukraine.

During our drive, I saw something on a Warsaw road in Poland that really stuck in my mind. What kept replaying in my mind was seeing a very small child standing at the side of a major road in Warsaw wanting to cross the very busy road. I don't know how or if she ever made it across to the other side, but if she did then that in itself would have been a miracle.

There is so much I could share about this three-week trip to the Ukraine and back, but time and space doesn't permit. The days were so full of God, so rewarding, and such a blessing. The four of us had a supernatural love for everyone we met, including the nice gentleman that had sealed up our vans at the checkpoint. On arriving back on the Isle of Man where Robert and I lived at the time, we were invited to tell our story in a radio interview, as well as for a newspaper article. It was a blessing to share what God had done.

All our time in the Ukraine visiting Chernobyl, giving medical equipment to grateful hospital staff, setting up the respite centre in Odessa, praying for sick people, and sharing the gospel of the Lord Jesus Christ made me want to be more and more involved in missionary work, helping people know about Jesus, and praying for those in need. I didn't know then, at that early stage of my Christian walk with God, that we are God's handiwork, created in Christ Jesus to do good works, which God prepared in advance for us to do (Ephesians 2:10). He has created us anew in Christ Jesus, so we can do the good things He planned for us long ago.

Psalm 21:2 says, "You have given him his heart's desire, and have not withheld the request of his lips". Now I understand that bit-by-bit God has been drawing me by His love and mercy and getting me to a place where my heart's request to be a soul saver and lifesaver would come to pass. God knew there were things that had to happen in my life before He could use me on the mission field. I am a willing vessel, Lord.

Chapter Three: Gladys Coutinho
Scotland, UK

Introduction from June Barron

I first met Gladys Coutinho at Rhema Scotland Church in Edinburgh. She was being prayed for by the pastor, Reverend Sherrie Hadden, who is greatly used in prayer for healing. I was blessed to spend a little time with Gladys and her sister Nancy as Gladys continued her fight against cancer. I was present when she was joined by an anointed young man from her native country of India who joined in the prayer fight for her healing. Gladys volunteered her family to host me if I travelled through Mumbai, and they helped me a great deal on several occasions. When she visited her family in Mumbai one year, she made a mission trip to our orphanage in Northeast India and met the folks involved.

Gladys paid for a medical camp at our mission and four surrounding villages, and she worked alongside the doctor and dentist. She was also taken by some of the young Indian ladies to minister in their town and village locations. As Gladys left us to return to her family in Mumbai, it was discovered that she had left behind enough medicines for a further two medical camps. I accompanied the doctors to reassure Gladys that her contribution was indeed fruitful. Gladys continued to pray and counsel via the Internet the young ladies she had made friends with, and indeed prayed for one young lady to find a husband.

Later that young lady married an American, and one day received ordination in the church in Edinburgh with Gladys attending to witness.

Gladys' Testimony

My name is Gladys Coutinho. I am a former nurse who loves Jesus. I was diagnosed with SECLAT cancer on 19 December 2008. As a result, I had severe toxicity from chemotherapy and radiotherapy, so the treatment was discontinued. I later underwent surgery, however, as a result of the treatment I suffered from surgical complications, and I still have a stomach bag. I was given six to eight months to live as a result of the chemotherapy and radiotherapy, but I survived the illness and was given an all clear by the doctors in the hospital in 2010 and returned to my nursing job.

In July 2019, I was diagnosed the endometrial cancer and underwent a total hysterectomy. The Lord gave me a piece of scripture from Isaiah 28:18 when I received the doctor's report. I am still standing on God's word, because they are filled with the Spirit and with life. Praise God I am still alive in 2021 and still standing in faith.

To God be the glory!

Chapter Four: Margo Doody
Republic of Ireland, EU

> Jesus, name above all names
> Beautiful Saviour, Glorious Lord
> Emmanuel, God is with us
> Blessed Redeemer, Living Word
> Lord I praise your name
> "Jesus the Name Above all Names" (by Naida Hearn)

My life began in a village in South Kilkenny, Ireland called Kilmacow. I was the youngest of three girls and grew up on a very pleasant farm in the midst of farm animals. My parents were Roman Catholics who prayed daily and liked to help neighbours, friends and family.

Sometime after my eldest sister Kathleen married, her husband Stephen became very ill. Though he had been going to doctors he wasn't getting any better. One day a friend named Elizabeth was at Kathleen's when Stephen collapsed in pain. Elizabeth prayed with him, and they managed to bring him to the hospital where he was immediately put into intensive care and given intravenous fluids, a nasogastric tube, et cetera. It's amazing when you are in the word of God how He looks after you. A fantastic senior doctor (Registrar) was down from Mater Hospital in Dublin for a year and was on duty the night Stephen was admitted. Stephen was diagnosed with acute pancreatitis and remained in hospital for a couple of weeks. When he was discharged, the consultants told him that after six months, and when he was stronger, he would have to return to Mater Hospital for an operation because x-rays showed a growth in his abdomen. Stephen returned to the hospital as directed and had the operation, but the consultant surgeons found nothing there. Thank God and the power of prayer.

A Healers' Touch

Elizabeth, her husband Maurice and I became great friends and would visit each other regularly. Before I started sharing stories about Elizabeth in this book, I asked permission from her husband, who is now ninety-two years old but still mobile and very alert. Maurice informed me that he would be happy if I wrote about her – I believe this is from God. There is much I could write about Elizabeth and how she helped people and prayed with them by the power of God. I am blessed to be able to share some moments.

Elizabeth and Maurice were both very faithful Christians. Elizabeth had a direct line to the Holy Spirit, and I would bring someone to her if they needed healing. When Maurice got acute leukaemia, Elizabeth said to God that if He healed her husband she would work for God the rest of her life, and she did.

> But Jesus looked at them and said, "With man it is impossible, but not with God; for with God all things are possible". (Mark 10:27)

God gave Elizabeth a salvation prayer to pray with people wherever she was. She often went to the town or outside the hospital to deliver people. I would like to share with you the prayer of commitment that she led them in as they turned their life over to the Lord:

> "Lord Jesus. I acknowledge that I am a sinner. I believe that You are the Son of God and that You died on the cross and forgave all my sins. I believe that God the Father raised You from the dead, and now Lord, I invite You into my heart to take over my life and rule it for me. Give me peace as my soul prospers, in Jesus' name. Amen".

The psalm that Elizabeth liked to pray for safety and abiding in the presence of God was Psalm 91. Elizabeth and Maurice also read other psalms daily and prayed the scriptures continuously.

Elizabeth was a very humble lady and was very friendly and helpful to everyone. She said to me that if someone does something to you or is unkind to you, you must pray for them and forgive them. I thought this was a very difficult thing to do but when I started to pray for these people, I soon realized how true it was. No more so than when my wrists were broken by a man who knocked me off my feet, and then fell on me in the tennis club. Some people said that he thought I was the ball. After recovering from surgery on my wrists, I went back to play tennis but felt a lot of pain until I forgave the man. After I forgave him, I had no more pain, thank God.

One evening, Elizabeth asked me to go to a meeting with her down to Rosslare. I brought a friend of mine who was a schoolteacher that had suffered from a breakdown and had been deserted by all her friends. She was healed completely that night and is still very healthy. I later gave her a Bible that she read through from cover-to-cover. Also, during the meeting, I was praying for my nephew who had just completed his Leaving

Certificate for school, and he thought that he had done very poorly. He was anxious to do medicine and, praise God, he got into medical school, flew through all his medical exams, and is a fabulous, kind and caring doctor. At the meeting, the visiting pastor was playing the guitar and singing Christian songs that were really nice. When he finished singing, he said that Jesus was walking around the room. I thought to myself, I do not see Him when all of a sudden I looked down and could see Jesus from the waist down (His white garment and sandals). I was instantly lifted up into heaven and felt really brilliant. In fact, I felt that way for a few weeks, until I gradually let the world in again.

> For the word of God is living and powerful, and sharper than any two-edged sword, piercing even to the division of soul and spirit, and of joints and marrow, and is a discerner of the thoughts and intents of the heart. And there is no creature hidden from His sight, but all things are naked and open to the eyes of Him to whom we must give account. (Hebrews 4:12–13)

As I write this, I am reminded of the song "He Touched Me", by Bill Gaither.

> Shackled by a heavy burden
> 'Neath a load of guilt and shame
> Then the hand of Jesus touched me
> And now I am no longer the same
> He touched, oh, He touched me
> And oh, the joy that floods my soul
> Something happened and now I know
> He touched me and made me whole
> Since I've met this blessed Savior
> Since He's cleansed and made me whole

> I will never cease to praise Him (to praise Him)
> I'll shout it while eternity rolls
> He touched me, oh, He touched me
> He touched me
> And oh, the joy that floods my soul
> Something happened and now I know
> He touched me and made me whole

My sister Kathleen brought Elizabeth to numerous family friends and neighbours for healing prayer by the power of God. Kathleen brought her to Mary (the sister-in-law of my other sister) who was healed of breast cancer after being prayed for by Elizabeth. And she brought Elizabeth to a family who had several members (even young ones) passing away with a rare heart disease that doctors could not diagnose. However, after Elizabeth prayed with them, they were sent to Mater Hospital to Doctor Mark Redmond, a renowned cardiac thoracic surgeon, who performed surgery and they are all healthy now, thank God.

Whenever I telephoned Elizabeth about a problem, by faith she would say that nothing would come of it. She was very anointed by God in praying for healing. When she prayed with a relative of mine whose baby was not growing in the womb, the baby was delivered perfectly normal, thank God. Another time, ladies who were told by their gynaecological doctors that their baby was abnormal went to Elizabeth for prayer. After she prayed with them, their babies were delivered perfectly normal.

One day at a prayer meeting in Wexford with Elizabeth, God gave one of the gentlemen at the meeting a song. When he left, I asked Elizabeth to say a prayer with me because I wanted to get a song from God. The song I got was "Away in a Manger", which we used to sing as children. I added a piece on and asked Jesus to come and live with me, and then one night I was speaking on the telephone in the sitting room when I saw a picture of Jesus on the floorboards. What an amazing God we have. Thank You, Lord Jesus. We worship You and give You all the honour and glory You deserve. God is light, love, and life (1 John 1:7).

Gone too Soon

Sadly, my friend Elizabeth passed away all too soon. A number of us were with her singing praise and worship songs the day before she passed. Even though she was very weak, she enjoyed them.

There were four miracles the day of Elizabeth's burial that could not be accounted for otherwise. The first miracle occurred when I left my house to go to the funeral Mass and burial. When I started out it was a beautiful fine day but a few miles down the road the heavens opened, and rain just poured down. Several days prior to this day, on a Saturday, my wipers had stopped working while on my way home from Enniscorthy after visiting Elizabeth. On the Monday, I went down to the Renault main dealership bright and early, but they could not fix them that day as they had to wait for the part to come from France. So, while driving to Mass I prayed continually, and the wipers continued to move as if there was nothing wrong with them.

The second miracle occurred when I arrived at the church for Mass. I got a parking space outside the church as it was early, and the service had not begun. After sitting in the church for about ten to fifteen minutes I started wondering where my car keys were. I suddenly realized that I must have left them in the car. I went out immediately to look and thanked God that they were still there in the car. What had happened was that I had put on my coat, which was lying on the back seat, and I had forgotten about locking the car door. That was completely out of character for me.

The third miracle occurred when I got to the burial ground. Rain poured out of the heavens, and that's when I discovered that the lovely, padded coat I had on was very warm but not suitable for rain. Every drop of rain went through the coat and penetrated to my skin. After the burial we went in for a meal at the request of the family. I took off my dripping coat and enjoyed the meal despite being soaked to my skin. When I got to the next town, I went into a shop to buy underclothes since the ones I had on were still wet. I never got a cold or felt any effects from the rain.

The fourth miracle was that my beautiful nephew Tommy was born by caesarean section on the same day as the burial with no problems, thank God. When Tommy's mother was pregnant with his older and younger sisters, she had pre-eclampsia (toxaemia). And during his younger sister's delivery, the gynaecologist cut an artery causing his mother to lose a number of pints of blood and requiring months to recover.

Jesus Beside Me

One night as I was on my way home from a Christian meeting that was quite a distance away, I was singing and praising God with a CD playing, and I could feel the presence of someone beside me in the car. As I was on the motorway, I had to wait before I could look around. I thought I must have left the car door open and someone got in, but when I looked I felt the presence of Jesus sitting beside me. I had been called to go to this meeting for a while but always said I could not go because of the frost and ice on the roads. When I did go, God thanked me with His presence.

Every night when my niece was pregnant with her baby, I was awakened to pray for them until the baby was born. She delivered the baby safely, thank God. The very next night I got an urgent unction from the Lord to pray, which lasted throughout the night, and I wondered who I was praying for now. The next day, I met someone who informed me that it was for one of my neighbours who had major surgery. Elizabeth had told me that she used to pray for people in tongues, so I asked God to use me in the same way.

> I will hear what God the Lord will speak,
> For He will speak peace
> To His people and to His saints;
> But let them not turn back to folly.
> Surely His salvation is near to those who fear Him,
> That glory may dwell in our land. (Psalm 85:8–9)

Scriptures poured into my heart affirming that the cross of Jesus is the power of God and that Jesus dying on the cross took away the sin of the world. Jesus who knew no sin became sin for us (2 Corinthians 5:21), and on the cross Jesus shed His blood for us seven times. Through the blood of Jesus, we can boldly enter into the presence of God because the curtain was torn from the top down.

> Behold, what manner of love the Father hath bestowed upon us, that we should be called the sons of God. (1 John 3:1 KJV)

> But if we walk in the light as He is in the light, we have fellowship with one another, and the blood of Jesus Christ His Son cleanses us from all sin. (1 John 1:7)

One night after a house meeting about fifty miles away from

my home, the pastor said that someone was getting a message, but no one got anything right then. I didn't get home that night until 2:00 a.m. but because the meetings were very powerful no one minded them going on longer. I had just sat down to a cup of herbal tea when I heard the loudest message from God that I have ever heard. Jesus was right beside me giving me a message for the pastor where I had just left. I had a book on the table with "JESUS" written in big letters on the front cover. Underneath His name was a crown, and underneath the crown it said, "Name Above All Names". On the bottom of the front cover was the author's name, Kenneth W. Hagin. I had gotten this book at a pop-up shop outside a Christian church from an African man the previous day and was just about to read it.

Israel

I have gone to Israel numerous times – whenever I get the chance actually. Every time I go, I get more of a love for it. You can feel the presence of Jesus all around, especially in Tiberias and the Sea of Galilee where Jesus worked a number of miracles and preached. In John 14:6, Jesus said, "I am the way, the truth, and the life. No one comes to the Father except through me". There is such peace in Israel and in Jesus.

In 2013, the year of recession, I telephoned everyone to see if they were going to Israel but received no response. Nevertheless, I knew God was calling me there, so I went to a travel agent to see the price of flights. I found that Turkish flights with a stop over in Istanbul were much cheaper, so I booked everything, including hotel only five days before departure. I came home delighted with myself but two nights before travelling I could not sleep and wondered what I had done because the previous year I could not find anything on my own. I got up the next day and said to Jesus, "If You are bringing me to Israel, You will have to show me everyplace as I cannot find anyplace on my own". When I got to Israel, I found everyplace with no problem. It was one of the best trips ever, thank God.

One year while at home, God said to me, "You have stayed long enough at this mountain". He wanted me to work at the Feast of Tabernacles in Israel. I had worked the festival a couple of times before and would happily do it again that year. The previous year, I was the only person from Ireland going so I thought this year I would again fly into Tel Aviv at 5:00 a.m. on my own. When I boarded the airplane at Heathrow Airport, my seat was at the back of the plane in the middle seat. I thought it was strange there were empty seats in my row as all the other seat rows on the plane were full. I had just spread out all my bags when along came two girls from the UK who I knew from previously helping at the Feast of Tabernacles. One of the girls had booked the window seat and the other the aisle seat. Not only were we flying together, but we were also going to the same hostel accommodation and could share. How good is our God?

One day during the trip, I went to a meeting in the En Gedi at the Dead Sea along with about five thousand other people. The area is desert country and really warm. After praise and worship, the preacher spoke a few words and said that every time he preached the Holy Spirit came. I was looking at the banner on the left-hand side of the stage when it crumpled up and blew down. I then looked at the banner on the right-hand side and it blew down. The preacher was now the only thing still standing on the stage when sand started blowing and it began raining, which is never heard of at the Dead Sea. The crowd started making their way to the buses, and so did I. As soon as I found my seat on the bus, a New Zealand man of about thirty years of age sat beside me. After driving a while, he felt to share with me that a couple of months previous he was waiting at the altar for his bride and watching her walking up the aisle when she had a brain haemorrhage and died. How devastating that must have been. We finally made it back to our hotel from the extraordinary day, and it was then when I saw the state of me. I looked in the mirror and saw that my hair was all matted together with sand and that my pink dress was full of sand. What a sight I must have been.

On the night before we went home from Israel, a friend asked if I would collect an item for her from one of the stalls where she had paid a deposit for it. I agreed since it was on my way to the meeting, so she gave me the amount of money it was going to cost. The artist could not remember getting the deposit, but I had been at this stall with my friend. We had bought praise and worship CDs that the artist had written herself, so I was convinced it was the right stall. The artist informed that she was only barely breaking even because it was very expensive to hire out the stall; however, I was delighted with my persistence in getting the item for my friend. When I got back to the hotel, my friend had already gone to bed so the next day when I gave it to her she was mortified because she had ordered a banner at a different stall. Nevertheless, everything worked out. I bought the painting from my friend, she got the banner she had originally wanted, and I sent the artist the deposit with a friend of hers. The painting was of a lion with a lamb's face. It's really beautiful and I have it hanging up now. I feel God was blessing this artist for her faithfulness to Him.

A few years ago, I was on a bus with a group of people in Jerusalem when torrential rain came down in buckets. Every place was flooded as the rain came down and severe thunder and lightning was all around us. This happened two successive evenings. We heard on the news that nine girls who had just graduated from college were on a short break before going into the army when they drowned in the flood. That night after a prayer meeting, a few of the people were panicking because we were leaving the next morning and going to Tiberias and Galilee. I thought to myself, we are sleeping there tomorrow night. Quietly, Psalm 121 came into my mind by the Holy Spirit, and I recited the psalm in its entirety. Everyone slept peacefully that night and returned to their usual cheerfulness the next day. We left early in the morning for our journey to Tiberias and Galilee, and it was a beautiful sunny day. We were blessed by God, and glorified God. His word says, "Your word is a lamp to my feet and a light to my path" (Psalm 119:105).

Every year we have a wonderful conference in Dundalk, Ireland in January that is organised by the International Christian Embassy Jerusalem. Speakers come directly from Israel to join Irish leaders. I usually got a lift with friends to the conference but about ten years ago nobody seemed to be going so I bought a satellite navigation system for my car. I bought it from an Australian man in an Irish shop. The Australian system seemed to be completely different from ours as they did not put in streets. I got ready to go to the conference and prayed and said to God, "If You want me to go, You will have to show me how to work the navigation system because I cannot do anything on my own". With God's help it worked, and I got to the conference, thank God.

One year, when I was three quarter way from the Dundalk conference, the snow came down heavily and quite a lot of snow settled on the road. I said to Jesus, "You know I cannot drive in frost and snow". So, I prayed in my heavenly language and the snow stopped and I could get through, thank God. One year, a niece of mine from one family was born during the conference, and another year a nephew of mine from a different family was born. God blesses me in so many ways.

In the year 2020, God asked the president and leaders of International Christian Embassy Jerusalem to organise a time of continuous prayer on the new moon, which is Rosh Chodesh. The event would be at least one positive outcome of the COVID-19 coronavirus crisis. Rosh Chodesh is a joyous festival given to Israel on Mt. Sinai. A blast of two silver trumpets signals the new moon and thus the new month (Numbers 10:10), and today marks the beginning of the month on the Hebrew calendar. In late May, the leaders in Jerusalem began thirteen hours of prayer and worship with leaders from different countries who wanted to join. In the month of June, the Rosh Chodesh prayer was a Zoom event that was broadcast around the world for twenty-four hours. Each country was allowed one hour for praise and worship. In August, it was forty-eight hours and in September it was seventy-two hours as more countries from around the world joined in. Isaiah 66:23 says, "From new moon to new moon, and from Sabbath to Sabbath, all flesh shall come to worship before me, declares the Lord" (ESV). All good things come from above.

God is preparing His people for the end times. More and more Jewish people want to make aliyah, which means to come back to Israel. More than one thousand Jews have gone home during the coronavirus epidemic, despite the recent global travel bans.

Final Thoughts

Oh, the blood of Jesus. The precious blood of Jesus. The

redeeming blood of Jesus, it washes white as snow. What can make me whole again? Nothing but the blood of Jesus.

I leave you with my final thoughts, which I express through beautiful melodies and songs that play in my heart. May God bless you and keep you and make His face shine upon you. And may God receive all the glory due His name through the prayers and testimonies of all His servants.

> "Oh the Love of My Lord Is the Essence" (by James Kilbane)
> Oh, the love of my Lord is the essence
> Of all that I love here on earth
> All the beauty I see He has given to me
> And His giving is gentle as silence.
> Every day, every hour, every moment
> Have been blessed by the strength of His love
> At the turn of each tide,
> He is there at my side,
> And His touch is as gentle as silence.
> There've been times when I've turned from his presence
> And I've walked other paths, other ways
> But I've called on His name in the dark of my shame
> And His mercy was gentle as silence
>
> "Holy Spirit" (by Bryan and Katie Torwalt)
> Holy Spirit, You are welcome here
> Come flood this place and fill the atmosphere
> Your glory, God, is what our hearts long for
> To be overcome by Your presence, Lord
> Your presence, Lord
> There's nothing worth more
> That could ever come close

No thing can compare
You're our living hope
Your presence, Lord
I've tasted and seen
Of the sweetest of loves
Where my heart becomes free
And my shame is undone
Your presence, Lord

Chapter Five: Brian and Jen Friend
England, UK

Introduction from June Barron

Brian and Jen Friend were my first teachers when I came to Christ. During my formative years I was supernaturally discipled and covered in prayer by them and their family, and indeed by the Alnwick Brethren. The Friends are Gideons, and much honoured members of the community. They are also leaders within Alnwick Baptist Church. Their son and daughter-in-law are co-pastors of that church. Brian and Jen have been faithful friends in the Lord for over forty years. I had asked them to take a look at my first book and I share their reply in this book because of a great testimony they included in their letter. The original source of the testimony and Wycliffe Bible Translators have given permission to share the story in this book. I believe it will be an encouragement to all.

Dear June,

Please forgive us for not returning your amazing book sooner. You have an awesome gift, and it's wonderful to see the way God is using you. Way back in the 1970's and 1980's I remember being so at awe that you really were Spirit taught, and it was a joy to see.

We do trust that yourself, Davy, and your family are all well and keeping free of this awful COVID-19 scourge. It's wonderful to see how the word of God is bringing huge good out of such a scary thing. All over the land (including locally) hospitals are asking Gideons for Bibles. And there was a wonderful story in a letter received from Wycliffe Bible Translators about a man named Sani, who used to be a Muslim and is now involved in Bible translation in Western Africa. He received a phone call from a Muslim man who said that he and four of his friends had recently experienced something extraordinary. The five men were all leaders of a militant group, and while taking 2,500 people to launch an attack the group had been confronted five times by a vision of a man in brilliant white. They went back to their camp and the man in white came again to the man who was making the phone call. He held out His hands and said, "I am Jesus. I have come that you might have salvation, and also to bring salvation to others". The militant leader immediately trusted Jesus as his Lord and his Saviour. Both amazingly and simultaneously the other leaders had also been visited by the man in white. They discussed what to do next and remembered hearing about Sani, a man who talked about Jesus in their own language. So, this man rang Sani and invited him to visit this militant group. After much prayer, Sani went to the camp.

There, Sani spoke to the 2,500 militants. Instead of preaching, Sani simply read scripture from the Bible, as the New Testament had been translated into both his and their own language a few years earlier. After reading scripture from four chapters in the Bible, Sani invited the men to accept Jesus. Amazingly, all 2,500 people who had previously launched the attack responded. Praise the Lord! This thrilled us to the core. Also, there are currently two thousand translations in progress, and more are waiting to start.

I know that the Wycliffe Bible Translators will have an objective of having some Scripture in every known language (over seven thousand, as I am sure you'll be aware), and that they will have it by 2025. I believe that they will do it. God bless you and yours June.

Much love from Brian and Jen

Chapter Six: Deborah Gaffney
Scotland, UK

During my trip to Jerusalem in 2019, I volunteered with Bridges for Peace (BFP), an organization of Christians supporting Israel. During my month of volunteering, I was based in Jerusalem. From the BFP base, I helped deliver food to local holocaust survivors as well as made distance bulk food deliveries to the Negev Region. What a wonderful time it was!

BFP is committed to educating and equipping Christians to identify with Israel, the Jewish people and their biblical/Hebraic foundations, and to bless Israel and the Jewish people in Israel and worldwide through practical assistance, volunteer service and prayer. Their goal is to communicate Christian perspectives to Israeli leaders and the Jewish community-at-large, to counter anti-Semitism worldwide and to support Israel's divine God-given right to exist in her God-given land. BFP has several programmes of practical helps that include food distribution, medical aid, new immigrant and Israeli town adoption, home repair and crisis assistance. Over 22,000 needy Israelis in forty communities are helped every month through BFP food banks in Jerusalem and Karmiel. It is a sign and a wonder when you think that BFP is only made up of a group of around fifty or so long-term individual volunteers and a few couples drawn from countries all over the world. The volunteers come from different cultures, different church denominations and different personal and professional backgrounds. They vary in age and experience, but the core uniting factor is their Christian faith and love for Israel. Despite all the seemingly incongruous combinations of personalities, there is an instant welcome and acceptance into the BFP family for every new volunteer, whether short- or long-term. God's blessing over BFP is very evident, and in fulfilment of Scripture that promises that those who bless His chosen people shall themselves be blessed.

During my 2019 trip to Jerusalem, I was part of a team that went out on monthly local food deliveries around various residential areas in Jerusalem visiting holocaust survivors (all in their eighties and nineties) We took a bag of essential food items to each one, which contained items like vegetable oil, flour, sugar, long-life milk, tinned vegetables and tuna, pasta and rice. We not only delivered food supplies, but we also checked to see that each person was well, and we spent a few minutes in their company. Many lived on their own and valued all human contact they had with any visitor to their apartment. Most only spoke Hebrew and their native language (commonly Russian). It was lovely to meet these precious people, but I had wished I could speak more Hebrew, as many couldn't speak English.

When helping BFP with bulk deliveries to the Negev Region, I was out first thing in the morning on a big truck loaded with three large pallets of food with Eli, the warehouse manager, who is an Israeli Messianic Christian Jew. The day was a delight from start to finish. Eli continuously talked about the areas we were travelling through, both in the context of biblical history and present-day life for Jews and Arabs. Our first stop was at Kiryat Malachi, where we offloaded the delivery from the pallet into the town's bomb shelter. A small group of Jewish volunteers distribute bags of supplies from there to needy individuals and families who were mostly new immigrants in the community. Our second stop was in Kiryat Gat at the home of an older Jewish couple who gave bags of food to those in need through various groups in their local area. The final stop was at Arad, a large town adjacent to the Dead Sea with scenery that is quite desert-like. The delivery point was at a warehouse with a café-type facility so that the people could come for hot food as well as take a bag of supplies away with them. The group who ran the distribution point came from all over the world – USA, Poland, Gaza, Pakistan. Such a friendly bunch; we laughed and chatted for quite a time over fresh cheese-filled pastries and coffee. There were hugs and photos all round as we departed. It was a great way to end our brilliant distance delivery day. As we returned to Jerusalem, we drove adjacent to the Green Line, which is a soft border between Israel and the West Bank (Judea and Samaria). The border fence is a necessary evil built by Israel for their own security. It is a high, concrete-slabbed, barbed wire-topped barrier stretching for miles and it is quite snake-like in places. There were a number of border crossing security points along the fence to monitor the entry and exit of vehicles twenty-four hours a day.

Not all my time was spent working with BFP. One particular day, the sun was shining in Jerusalem in the early evening as a friend and I made our way from Succat Hallel (Tabernacle of Praise) up the winding path to the Zion Gate and through the streets of the city to the Western Wall. We merged into a crowd on the same path to celebrate the start of Shabbat (sundown Friday till sundown Saturday). The left side of the Western Wall is reserved for men and the right side for women. We watched as circles of celebratory Jews danced round with arms entwined, singing joyful songs on both sides of the divide. Many others made their way to the wall to pray. As the sun set, swifts were flying and calling, darting to and fro above the heads of the happy throng, then squeezing into the crevices in the Western Wall to nest for the night. Finally, the floodlights came on, making the scene even more atmospheric. What a special and memorable experience this was!

I returned to Jerusalem the next year (2020) and volunteered once again with BFP. The second trip turned out to be nothing like my experience in 2019. My personal scripture on my first day in Jerusalem during this trip was James 1:12, "God will bless you, if you don't give up when your faith is being tested" (CEV).

As I began my time in Israel, the coronavirus pandemic was ramping up all over the world. Only a few days in, authorities were already beginning to bring in restrictions on gatherings and freedom of movement for the population across the country. After a week, I was told that the government had decided that everyone in Israel on a tourist visa could be required to leave the country at short notice. That was quite a bombshell and out of the blue. Thankfully, this directive did not materialise in the end, and I was able to stay.

Despite the fact that I was the only foreign volunteer at BFP at that time, they allowed me to come even though they didn't really need me. Every morning that the food bank team met at the warehouse it started with an update from the government website about the ever-tightening restrictions that would impose upon BFP operations. Face masks, gloves and antiseptic wipes were distributed to all, and we had to abide by the rules for social distancing and travel arrangements. The restrictions started to severely hamper and curtail our activities in certain respects. Our major concern was for the needy and vulnerable people who we desperately wanted to continue to support.

We managed to adapt some of our procedures regarding food distribution to ensure that the supplies continued, but we missed so much the direct and personal contact with the people themselves. We realised that this was so intrinsic to the ministry of BFP in Israel. It is not just about provision but also about connection – showing the love of Messiah Yeshua to His own chosen people through personal interaction.

As the days went on, things became more difficult. We were advised not to take public transport, but to walk to the assistance centre from our apartment in the morning and home at the end of the day to cut down the risk of contamination. Non-essential shops and malls were closed down, and the airport was closed to all incoming flights. The tourist industry virtually ground to a halt, and the livelihood of many who relied on it for their source of income was seriously threatened. Supermarkets were overcrowded and understocked, and there was a sense of fear and desperation in the air.

Amidst all this, BFP doggedly stuck to doing as much as possible to fulfil the needs of those who were relying on them for necessities. Some new arrivals to Israel, having made aliyah from foreign lands, had been adopted into the new immigrant scheme. So, we donned our masks and gloves, and took bags of essential supplies to their apartments, knocked on the door and left the bags outside for collection. Under normal circumstances, the adoptees would come to the assistance centre to collect supplies, but nobody was allowed into the building apart from the food bank workers.

Ten days after my arrival in Israel, I received an email from the airline that I was booked with saying they had cancelled some of their flights, and I needed to rebook mine. This caused major difficulties because I was unable to get through on the twenty-four-hour helpline, even in the middle of the night. A few days later, I received another email saying that they were suspending all their flights until further notice. This trauma lasted around a week before it was resolved, and my faith was really tested in so many ways in the interim. James 1:12 was truly my scripture.

In the meantime, total lockdown was announced by government authorities, and all of us at BFP were confined to our apartments with only Zoom meetings and WhatsApp to keep us connected. I spent most of the last week of my stay effectively on my own, with short bursts of fresh air and exercise around the block a couple of times a day to keep my body and mind in some semblance of functionality.

With much prayer and practical support, God came through for me. He got me out of the country on the last suitable scheduled flight from the almost deserted Tel Aviv Airport before a complete airport shutdown took effect.

This trip was a learning experience in so many ways. All the glory goes to God for His grace abounding toward me throughout. The last entry in my journal diary was, I think, my most significant entry of the whole time I spent in Israel in 2020:

> Return to the Homeland!
> As I was out for a morning walk, the day before I am due to fly back to the UK, I was pondering my feelings about it all.
> It occurred to me that, in a time of crisis or extreme uncertainty or disruption, foreigners abroad turn their thoughts back to their native land.
> Even within the country of birth or upbringing, an emergency instinctively draws someone home. I have never thought of the UK in terms of my place

of safety, security, and comfort until now. Now I have a confirmed flight back to London tomorrow, I am truly looking forward to being back on home turf, so to speak.

As I continued in this train of thought, I aligned it with God's chosen people making aliyah back to Israel. I believe there will be huge increases in immigration back to Israel for the Jewish people from now on. Not only is the tide of anti-Semitism continually building worldwide, crises like COVID-19 will be ongoing and increasing in intensity as we grow closer to the return of Yeshua Ha Mashiach to Jerusalem to establish His millennial throne. On that great and glorious day, they will rise together and declare with one voice, "Baruch haba, B'Shem Adonai! (Blessed is He who comes in the name of the Lord!)".

Chapter Seven: Premdan Majhi
Northern Ireland, UK

My name is Premdan Majhi. At present, I live in Northern Ireland, however, I was born and brought up in India in a Christian family. God's hand has been upon me throughout my life and continues even now. I would like to share with you the years of growing up with my family. My parents were originally from an animistic background before they became followers of Jesus Christ. My granddad, my dad and his siblings were completely devoted to worshiping the creation. They would hold animistic worship meetings once a month that would sometimes last a whole week. In addition to their devotion to animism, the saddest thing was that my parents had no children.

My mum told me that she was treated very badly in the family because she was barren. My mum and dad felt so miserable and hopeless. During that time a preacher came to their home and shared the gospel of Jesus, in particular the book of Samuel. He told the story about Hannah praying for a son and telling God that if her prayer was answered she would give her son back to Him. The scripture touched my mum and she believed in the power of Jesus. Both my parents gave their lives to Jesus that same day. The preacher prayed over them and told them to believe that Jesus would do miracles in their lives. Guess what happened next – a baby boy was born the following year and the same preacher named the baby Premdan. Yes, that was me. I was the answered prayer of my mum.

I was around five years old when I realized that my dad was preaching in the church in our village called Leesh River Tea Garden. My dad was an ordained pastor, and the congregation was affiliated with Church of God. To cut the story short, my parents had a big influence on me spiritually and in my walk with the Lord Jesus since my childhood. They would always remind me that I was born because of their prayers, and that they had dedicated me to the service of the Lord. However, in spite of growing up in a Christian family I went astray from God when I was a teenager. As a teenager, I was in bad company with all my friends, drinking and fighting. I joined this bad company because of peer pressure. I had no friends in my village because my dad was very strict with his rules at home, like praying every evening, going with my parents to house meetings every evening, and reading Scripture in house fellowships and in the Sunday service.

My dad tried to keep me from the influence of the bad boys in the village who would not go to school but spent their time drinking and smoking from an early age. There were no other Christian children in my village. I felt very upset because I had no friends at all. At the age of fifteen, I became rebellious and joined the bad company of boys. The boys used to tease me because I didn't drink or smoke. They would taunt me saying, "Prem you are a good boy, a non-smoker, non-drinker and a son of a pastor. You can't join us because we are bad boys, so go away". I would say to them, "Hey! Do not worry. I am ready to smoke with you all". So, I started smoking and drinking with them to be accepted. I was with those guys for about two years smoking, drinking and fighting when I was sixteen to seventeen years old. When I turned eighteen years old, God started working in my life by making me realize that I was doing wrong.

He reminded me of all the words of God that I had learned in Sunday school and in church when my dad was preaching. One afternoon I was lying on my bed when suddenly tears started to roll down my cheeks. I was sobbing for a couple of hours as the Holy Spirit was convicting me of my wrongdoing and bringing me to repentance. After two hours of weeping, I talked to my parents and asked for forgiveness. I also told them that I wanted to go away from my village to study, far from the bad company so that I would not be influenced by them anymore.

My mum and dad agreed to my proposal as they also wanted me to turn away from the world, be a good boy and give my life to Jesus. I was sent to a beautiful hill station called Darjeeling for my study. It was there in Darjeeling that I confessed from my mouth at the age of eighteen that Jesus is my Saviour and the Lord of my life.

After six months of being in Darjeeling, I heard some shocking news about one of my old friends. The guy that I used to be with most of the time was killed by some other gang. It was shocking to me because before I came to Darjeeling one other boy in the bad group had told me and the friend who was killed that someday one of us would either kill somebody or be killed. That incident let me know that God's hand was on me all through the time. God picked me out of this bad company and saved my life at the right time or else I may have been in the place of the guy who was killed.

After that incident, my faith and passion for Jesus started to grow stronger. God started telling me that He had not only saved me, but He had also chosen me to be an ambassador of Christ. I then decided to go to a Bible institute to study and devote myself to the word of God. In 2002 I started a three-year period of attending the Bible institute. I saw many signs and the power of God manifest during those years. During the winter holidays at Bible school, I used to follow my dad when he went to villages to share the gospel of Jesus. I could really see the power of God manifest in the villages through our lives, and as a result people came to faith and gave their lives to Jesus.

I would like to share an incident that happened in one of the villages. There is so much witchcraft in the remote villages of India. My dad and I happened to go to a village where there was a man who was demon possessed. The man had been a shy person and very well mannered but after being possessed he became very violent. He tried to attack villagers and family members with a knife or anything he had in his hand. His family had to tie him with thick ropes to a pole inside the house. My dad and I used to go to the other side of the village to share about Jesus and His power to transform lives. One Sunday we were in a house talking about Jesus when two people came to us and said that there was a man on the other side of the village who had become mad and very violent. They asked us whether the God we were preaching about could heal this man. My dad said yes, that in the name of Jesus every sickness is healed, every demon is cast away, and nothing is impossible with him who believes in Jesus.

We were taken to the home of the man's parents. His parents were full of tears looking at us and requesting us to pray for their son. Before we prayed, my dad shared the gospel of Jesus with the family and also with the neighbours who had come there to see us. We asked the family to have faith in Jesus and He would heal their son. The family said they would believe in Jesus, so we prayed for the demon-possessed son. We rebuked the demon in the name of Jesus that Sunday and told the family that we would come back the next Sunday. To be honest, we were so restless the whole week thinking about that possessed man we had prayed for. It was a big challenge for us ministering before those village people, as they were waiting to see this man delivered. The entire week we had been praying to God to manifest His healing power. It was the year 2003 so people in the villages did not have any phones to contact anyone so we had no knowledge of what was going on there.

The next Sunday we arrived at the village and saw that some people were gathered outside the man's house waiting for us. My dad and I were a bit worried to see the crowd. We started to pray to God even more in our hearts that everything was good with the man. When we came closer to the crowd they cheered aloud and said the man was completely healed. Actually, the demon-possessed man was healed the Monday after we prayed for him. The delivered man was now preparing a meal for us, as we came from a far away village for the entire day to preach the gospel. The man's deliverance was a big manifestation of the power of God in that village. Afterwards, neighbours also started to believe in Jesus and soon gave their lives to Him.

There are so many miracles like this that happened in India. The power of our Lord Jesus was constantly confirming that His power is greater than any power in the world. Praise His name! He never lets us down.

My God did not only manifest His power through healing and miracles in our ministry in India, but He was also interested in my personal life. In 2010 He brought a beautiful girl right in front of me in India from the far away country of Ireland. We married on 23 August 2011. After we married, we moved to Northern Ireland. It was a completely different environment for me, but I believe that it was God's plan for us to move to Ireland. God has opened the door for me to preach the gospel and reach out to people there in many different ways.

At the moment I have been leading a Bible study group in Northern Ireland and people are being blessed by the word of God. I believe God has even more to do in and through our lives here in days to come. I have so many things to share but I can't write everything in this testimonial. I believe that by reading what God has been doing in and through our lives you will be encouraged and be blessed as well.

Thank you and God bless you.

Chapter Eight: Thelma Pallas
England, UK

June 18, 2020

My lockdown began before COVID-19. My husband, Ron, received a diagnosis of terminal fibrosis at Easter the previous year. As he became weaker, he needed me to be there for him in the house, so I only went out for absolute necessities. There was so much extra to do, nights were disturbed and often I felt exhausted. And then, one day I got a letter from a friend in France. Across the top of the page were the words, "He gives strength to the weary", as referring to Isaiah 40:29. That was just what I needed, and that was just what I received in so many different ways – each time with the reminder that God is God and all that it implies. There is no end to what He can do.

In those last days of Ron's life, God provided everything we needed – help during the day from our wonderful church family and help at night from hospice care workers. Toward the end, the presence of our two daughters and their daughters, and each of their nursing skills and all their loving care made such a difference.

Over the days following the funeral, all the family gathered and our young people became much more aware of each other. When the details of paperwork and financial arrangements became burdensome, and the cleaning of drawers, wardrobes, and cupboards threatened to overwhelm us with memories, we continually reminded ourselves that God is God. He will be our help and strength, and nothing is too difficult for us if our trust is in Him.

As a loving Father, God has to repeat often what He has said to us in the past – His words about giving strength to the weary in Isaiah 40:28–31. I used verse 30 as basis for testimony years ago, "Even youths grow tired and weary, and young men stumble and fall; but those who hope in the Lord will renew their strength. They will soar on wings like eagles; they will run and not grow weary; they will walk and not be faint" (NIV).

I found those words encouraging, though in those days I had never done any soaring. But now I am soaring as I am so aware of God's power to hold, to enable, to supply and to fulfil every promise of His word. I am so full of thankfulness for all that is passed, and I am full of hope for what is to come.

One Sunday, in response to a text message, I opened my front door and found on the doorstep a box with some fresh broad beans inside. I was preparing lunch, so I popped them into boiling water and cooked them for my meal. They were delicious. As I was enjoying them, I began to think of other things that turned up on my doorstep.

Each morning my paper is delivered, and the postman calls just as regularly. It's easy to take their faithful service for granted. Another welcome visitor was the window cleaner – there was no problem with social distancing for him!

Some callers are very special, like the person who brings my weekly shopping requirements and people who just knock and ask if there is anything I need. Some people just come by for a chat. They either wave from the street to attract my attention, or they ring the doorbell and distance themselves to the road while I stand on the doorstep to chat. I thoroughly enjoy their company.

Sometimes I put my rubbish out on the step for collection as the bins are at the end of the street. And every week I put my letter out in a plastic folder for Carol, who takes it off to post.

The best caller who has ever come to my door was the one that came in 1947. He said, "Here I am! I stand at the door and knock. If anyone hears my voice and opens the door, I will come in and eat with him and he with me" (Revelation 3:20). That caller was Jesus, and I answered, "Yes, please come in", and I've never regretted it.

This time of lockdown and restriction has not been a lonely time but a lovely time with the Person who is always there and with whom I have everything I need. I hope He is your companion too.

Chapter Nine: Richard John Perry
Scotland, UK

Mission India, 2016

It was 2016 and I was going about life as normal, working, fellowshipping with friends, going to church, et cetera. That year I decided it would be a wise financial decision to change my mortgage. In doing so, I ended up with £1,300 coming back to me so I asked the Lord what He wanted me to do with the money. In an unexpected response, He said, "Go to India". The Lord's response was one I quite willingly received, as I had friends in India who had been asking me to come, and I desired to be obedient to the Lord's call.

Having known the Reverend. June Barron through church for quite awhile, I had by now heard many testimonies, both from behind the pulpit and in fellowship, of her mission work across India. This God-appointed relationship set in action my trip to India, so I decided to join June on her next trip. She arranged all the travel details, with all the flights coming to just over £600 (ten flights in total).

My friend Sam Appollos and his father, who live in India, had been praying for me and for others to come and minister God's word to the people in India. After travelling over twenty-four hours, I was met by Sam at the Madurai Airport in the state of Tamil Nadu and was then taken to his father's home where I stayed for a week. Sam said that he would pay for everything on the trip as I, along with others, had looked after him for two years when he had attended Bible school in Scotland.

The evening of my arrival, I was taken to a pastor's meeting. I would like to share with you that I had never spoken to a group of pastors before, and, in fact, while in school I felt that me speaking in front of others was virtually impossible. However, now I found myself in front of a group of pastors to preach not just once but twice. The first message I gave was about Abraham preparing to sacrifice His son Isaac as told in Genesis 22, and the second message was about Ruth the Moabite.

A few days later we drove to a village in India and stayed one night in a hotel. The next day I would be speaking at a young church led by Pastor R and attended by mostly gypsies. Before leaving in the morning, the Lord told me to put a t-shirt on and also a smart shirt. Sam was wondering what I was doing with two shirts on, as it was very warm. God knew why.

We arrived at Pastor R's church but before I spoke Sam and I met with the pastor. We then walked to the site where the parishioners of this young church were building a new church structure on land that had been given to them. Many people had previously prayed over the land asking for God's blessing to be upon the church. Consequently, this new church building was as a result of all the prayer. As I walked into the church structure, I could feel that God's presence and an open heaven was already there. The Holy Spirit came upon me, and I began to pray. I started speaking prophetically, and then prayed for Pastor R. I then took the smart shirt off and placed it upon his shoulders, as the Lord led me to do.

We walked back to the temporary church building to begin

the meeting. I firstly spoke out of my spirit, and then I taught out of the book of Ruth. Like Ruth, Pastor R and many in his church were orphans, also. My friend Sam commented about how well I had spoken out of the love of a father's heart for his people. After I had preached, many people came to me for prayer. One moment that really touched my heart was a young girl, age maybe thirteen or so, who came with her older friend. The young girl wanted my blessing, so I prayed for her and at the end of the prayer she then called me father. At this, I put my arms across her shoulders and gave her a small hug, and tears started to flow down the young girl's face. Later that day as Sam and I were travelling back home recalling all that happened, Sam said that most of the young children at that church had never experienced the true love of the Father. God truly knows what His children need.

For the next part of my time with Sam, he took me to meet a gentleman named Martin. Martin was a pastor who had never retired. Martin's family was living in the flat above Sam, and they were Hindus. Because Martin was a Christian, a family member decided to put poison in his food. Martin became very sick and fell in the street while walking. When a passer-by saw him in the street, they rushed Martin to the hospital. It was quickly diagnosed that he had been poisoned, and it was determined that the family member responsible had suddenly died. Martin was slowly getting back to normal when Sam and I came to see him. After speaking for a little while, we prayed for Martin at his request. At the end of the prayer, Martin went and got some gifts and in doing so said, "When you bless those who God sends, then God in return blesses you". He gave me some sweets, a very smart shirt and a shawl that he placed upon my shoulders. I learnt later that in Indian customs placing clothing on another person's shoulders means you're honouring that person. After we left the hospital, Sam and I agreed that Martin's eyes were much brighter, and his face was radiant.

Before leaving India, I was able to visit the orphanage and mission centre in Northeast India that is the work of God being accomplished through June's ministry. While there, I met a young man named Savington who asked me to pray for his neck. He had previously hurt his neck very badly while doing farming work on the mission centre land, and he couldn't move it without a lot of pain. He was not sleeping very well as every time he moved his neck it would get even more painful. I place my hand upon his neck and prayed. Though neither Savington or I felt any change at the time, the next day he came back to give me some very nice bananas and said that his neck had been totally healed. Praise God!

Revival Sites, 2019

In late June 2019, I was invited to a ministry conference at the Bible College of Wales founded by Rees Howells in Swansea, South Wales. During the conference we spent one day visiting Welsh revival sites. It was such a blessing to visit places where the Lord poured out His presence. I believe that He today is reopening those wells that had once brought blessing upon His people all over the world. It has been estimated that from the wells of the Pentecostal outpouring of God's Spirit in Wales over 800 million people have since then been touched by that move of God's Spirit.

One afternoon, the ministry conference team went to Moriah Chapel in Loughor, which is the place where the Welsh Revival started. We sang some old hymns and had the opportunity to ask the chapel attendant questions about the chapel and its history. We also took holy communion together during which we were all asked to pray by Reverend June. As we did this, we got a very strong feeling of God's presence in the building, as if Jesus was in the room with us right in front of our faces. I've experienced a touch of God's holiness on a few occasions, and this was such an occasion.

COVID-19 Healing, 2020

As the world knows, 2020 was the year that a coronavirus called COVID-19 hit the nations. A few months into the year, I was speaking to an old friend of mine who I've known for over twenty-five years and is a pastor in a church in Birmingham, England. He had told me that he had all the symptoms of COVID-19 and had them for about twenty-one days. As a result, he was in great pain and was finding it difficult to breath. As I was speaking with him on the phone he asked if I could pray for him. I prayed in faith standing on God's promises, and within a few days all the pain and symptoms had gone, and my friend was back in good health. All glory goes to our God, our Healer.

All my thanks go to the Lord.

Chapter Ten: Barbara Pollard
England, UK

Doors Opening

A man I know who lives just outside of York, England came one Sunday to the church I attended. We talked together after the service, and he told me about what was happening in India with a lady named June Barron from England. He asked me if I would like to go to a retreat on the Isle of Man where June would be speaking. I wanted to go, as I had never been to the Isle of Man, but I was booked in for summer school at a Bible college in Swansea, South Wales and I didn't have the money go to both. The following Monday, the man phoned and said, "I have booked you in for the retreat on the Isle of Man, where you will hear and meet June Barron, a missionary to India". The summer school in Wales was a few weeks later so I would have to be very careful financially to manage both. I enjoyed the retreat and met June, as well as some other lovely people from India, Isle of Man, Ireland, USA and the UK, and also David Hathaway from South Africa. The hotel owner was a lovely Christian man.

At the retreat, we gathered each morning in a large oblong room with chairs positioned all around the edge of the room. On the Tuesday morning, a fair-haired lady came into the room, laid her bag on a seat, and then walked over to me. She handed me an envelope, and said, "Jesus said you need this. Don't say anything more about it", and then went back to her chair. It wasn't until evening when I went to my room that I looked inside the envelope to see £200. Wow! That would take care of the hotel bill and pay for the summer school fees. My husband had worked at the railway, so I had a free train pass to travel to Wales. God is good as we step out in faith. He provides all we need and more.

After I returned home from the retreat, I went buzzing back to my church with a testimony of God's wonderful provision of covering the expenses for the retreat and summer school. I then invited a friend to come to summer school and told her that if she could manage the train fare and I would pay the school fees. Of course, she said yes. We gathered lots of teaching at the school, and it was a wonderful experience for us.

I met June on more than one occasion after the Isle of Man, at conferences in Ireland and England. One time she was speaking in Hull, England and needed bed and breakfast for the night so she stayed with me in Haxby in York. We sat talking until 2:00 a.m., sharing our life stories with each other. She told me of her call to India and we talked about the similarities in our times. Before we went to bed she asked if I would go to India and teach the children there on the streets and paths. So, I began to pray about going to India. What worried me most was the required finances because I had no spare money, as my husband died years before.

Struggles Turned into Blessings

My husband Eddie had been sick for twenty-two years. We loved God deeply and trusted Him for money and other things when times were tough. Eddie and I ran a Sunday school together in School Hall at Tang Hall in York. We had approximately forty to fifty children, half of whom were boys who went to Eddie's class. We divided the girls into groups and we young women taught them on Wednesday evenings. The classes were filled with children from where Eddie and I lived. We drove them to the church, singing songs that the children loved while on the way. The devil is a sly old fox – if I could catch him, I'd put him in a box, turn the lock and lose the key for all the tricks he has played on me (I'm glad I've received salvation twice). The children would sing so loud when we travelled home. We drove with the windows open so I'm sure all could hear a happy choir of boys and girls (our two boys included).

I often hadn't all the money to pay the bills – usually the electric bill. – so, I took a job. A local businessman named Walter gave me a job posting envelopes through house doors, and then collecting them to raise money for people with heart problems. As pay, I received 10% of the money collected. I had two weeks to deliver and collect the envelopes while filling in for Walter, who had a pacemaker operation.

One day Walter rang and said that his typist had given up her job. He asked if Eddie and I would like to hand write 1,000 envelopes for him for one penny an envelope. What an answer to prayer this was as a week before our oven had died. I had my eye on an oven that was on sale at the electric shop but didn't know how we would pay for it. On a Friday morning, Eddie decided we would buy the oven (at the expense of the electric bill again). Immediately, we went to the electric shop and put £13.26p down as a deposit. When we came out of the shop, there was Walter. He said, "God told me you needed the money for writing the envelopes now. I was just coming to your house to give you it". With that, he gave us £10 in advance for all the envelopes to be written and 2 shillings for each to be delivered.

With that money, we only had to add pennies out of my purse towards the deposit.

God continued helping us over the next few years. During two Christmases, we received £10 notes in Christmas cards, not knowing who sent them. One Christmas, I told Eddie that we only had money for a small chicken for Christmas dinner. A few days later there was a knock on the door from a man who felt to bring us a turkey for Christmas dinner. Then nearer to Christmas day, I went out to get the milk bottles delivered outside the front door and found a turkey on the door mat. I froze it and we had it for New Year's Day dinner.

One year, when Eddie was in hospital to have another operation on his back, I had to tell him that we were having a baby. Our two boys were eleven and fifteen years old when the following year another baby boy was born. God provided lots of baby clothes, though a pram was all I needed for a new baby. My missionary friends from Ghana sent me some baby sleep suits, which I never had for my other babies.

Called to India

Years had passed and Eddie died. I was reading through the Bible daily and had reached 1 Chronicles 4:10, "And Jabez called on the God of Israel saying, 'Oh, that You would bless me indeed, and enlarge my territory, that Your hand would be with me, and that You would keep me from evil, that I may not cause pain!' So, God granted him what he requested". That verse stood out, so I wrote it on a paper and put it on my bedside cabinet so that I could read it every time I saw it. At the time, I was running Sunday school and began to tell the children that I might be going to India. Suddenly, they started bringing me some of their pocket money towards the trip. And then miraculously, I had a young friend down south who sent me her first fruits of £40 in obedience to God. Other people started giving me money until and it soon reached £2,000, enough to get me to India and some to bless Indian pastors.

In March 2007, I was off to India as part of June's mission team. My sister and pastor's wife travelled with me to Heathrow Airport, where I joined another lady from Ireland who was part of the mission team. When taking the underground train, I sat near an Indian man and told him that I was going to India – he gave me two Indian rupee notes. Then, when going down the elevator an Indian man behind me saw that my cases were heavy, so he gave me his brief case to carry instead. One of my cases was full of baby clothes, a shawl crocheted by a friend, asthma trumpets, wallets, diabetes test kits, teddy bears and a little cash. The second case contained my clothes. We all felt it was an angel who traded cases with me, as who would trust you with their briefcase?

The lady and I arrived at Delhi International Airport, and then had to walk to the domestic airport where we would fly to Meghalaya in Northeast India. On the walk, we saw a scruffy man begging for money. Upon arriving in Meghalaya, we were greeted by many Indians happily welcoming us. We were driven to June's mission house where we met Moon, an Indian boy. Moon came from a family with ten children. His father had only one eye and his mum was very young. June provided Moon a home, food, clothes and an education in return for him staying at and caring for the mission house. Moon did the food shopping and cooked for us the English way when we came back from visiting shacks where families lived.

I must say, transportation in India is an adventure in itself! On the highways, there are many high-sided lorries with brightly painted patterns on their sides. The roads are bendy, and the people drive on any side of the road (even down the middle sometimes) beeping their horns a few times to announce they are coming through. At night it is no different, except that often times a truck's headlight is blown out– sometimes both headlights – making it hard to see the truck coming. One day, a pastor asked me if I would like to drive. I half jokingly said that it would take us another few hours to get there if it was dark.

One morning we needed to return to the mission house from a different location so rather than drive several hours down winding rough roads, we took a helicopter. Walking onto the helipad there were soldiers with guns who asked me to open my case. I rolled the numbers on the lock, but it wouldn't open. After unsuccessfully trying a few times, the soldier quite sternly told me to me to go ahead to the helipad. I was afraid to get into the helicopter as it was old and rattly, but off I went over some bleak mountainous areas to the next location. When we got home to the mission house, the men had to break the lock to open the case.

The mission house had a lovely maroon vehicle that belonged to June. As we drove the roads, we would see little stalls with lots of people walking around them. One evening, I noticed a stall that had an electric light bulb hanging in the middle of it for light, and Indians selling sweets, drinks and vegetables. During the day you would see women with vegetables to sell at the end of the main roads. One day we were taken to a bakery that was just a small place that had a large fire and oven at the side. It was a family business that made biscuits. The children were about ten or eleven years old, and they helped make the biscuits. In most homes that you go to in India, the people give you a cup of tea and a biscuit when you sit down to visit. Outside the bakery were four small black goats. We didn't see many animals apart from cows in the cities, which at the time were sacred in India.

A local pastor would drive us to villages where he would visit the parents of the children, while we told stories of Jesus to the children. The children would come outside on the paths each time we stopped in an area that we walked to. I had a hand puppet that I had knitted named Lamb Choppy that I used mostly for the Lost Sheep story. The children were afraid of the puppet until I stroked its face so they could see it didn't hurt me. I used flannel graphs and colourful felt figures of animals, buildings and scenery to tell Bible stories. At the end of the story, I would ask if they would like to give their hearts and lives to Jesus, and many did.

Another local pastor took us to a Christian school in an area that looked like Scotland, with tall pine trees and water brooks. There were between sixty to seventy children ages three to fifteen years at the school who came in on buses. The morning we arrived, the children were outside the school under a tree saying the Lord's Prayer in English. The children were taught English at the school. The head mistress then gave me ten minutes to tell a story. The children stood quietly as I told a story using the flannel graphs. When I finished, I looked at the head mistress and she asked if I had another story. I told the story of Noah, using a book bag that you keep turning inside out. The head mistress asked for yet another story, so I used Lamb Choppy to tell the story of Lost Sheep. The children responded when I said we are like lost sheep and Jesus is the Shepherd looking for you to say yes to Him and not be lost, and to be forgiven. The children stood in rows; the very small ones stood with a finger over their lips and were quiet. I suggested they put their hands up in the air and we would pray and doing so I asked them to repeat after me a prayer to Jesus. We just knew God was there with us and that He did something beautiful with the children. Afterwards we were given a meal, and then asked to write in a book something from the Bible, which everyone who visited the school did. There were so many Bible verses written in it, it was like opening a handwritten Bible. I wrote a verse from 1 Corinthians.

After our time at the school, we were taken along a path to a prayer room that was open for anyone to go in and pray. As we walked up to the building, we saw cross shaped windows from the side to the doorway. The people there had saved pennies until they had enough money to build the prayer room. We were asked to take off our shoes as we went inside. In the downstairs room, I felt God's presence so strong I just fell on my knees. There was a metal ladder used to climb onto the second floor where there was an area to sit on the floor to pray. We climbed the ladder and sat for a while quietly. There were two young Indian men in the room with us when the pastor asked if I had a word for the two men. One of the men was married and only saw his wife one Saturday every two weeks as she ran girl's home. If she came to work with him, the girls in the home would be on the streets because it was too far away for them to travel. The other young man longed for a wife. God's word for this young man was to treasure Him and that in time God would bring him a wife.

As we drove back to the mission house, we visited two girls who were sponsored by some people in York. I couldn't stop crying when I saw the girls, who kept hugging me and telling me not to cry. We had just seen a twelve-year-old boy and his two nephews living in a shack that had a roof that leaked. Their uncle had to find small animals to kill and cook on the fire for the children because their parents had died. The twelve-year-old was also sponsored by York people. All of the boys were wearing English trousers with broken zips, and I said that when I came again, I would bring some safety pins. Meanwhile, I left some money for a new shack to be built for them in the village near the school where the twelve-year-old went to school.

Each day we would travel miles away with a pastor to areas where he visited parents and families. While the pastor ministered to them, he said to just wait on the paths and that children would come – and they did. In each area more than twelve children would appear. It was exciting seeing them respond to the love of Jesus and giving their lives to Him. I asked the pastor if there was a sick baby to give the shawl to that my friend had crocheted. The pastor said that a new baby had been born a few days before, so I gave the shawl to him for the baby. One Sunday we were taken to a home and land of an Indian man who had built a church on his land, at his own expense. That Sunday I was asked to speak at the service without advance notice and spoke on Psalm 46.

Another evening we met for a conference in a big meeting hall that was very dark inside. At the meeting there were men who had been head-hunters only 100 years earlier but were now Christians. The men presented each of us with a handmade Naga shawl and placed it around our shoulders. Mine was black with diagonal gold flashes and red elephants. I remember feeling how generous they were to us. One of the pastors came down with malaria and the people used all their money to pay for him to go into hospital. Seventeen of us went to see him and prayed with him, asking God to heal him. The pastor was to lead the opening meeting on the Friday evening of the conference, but he was very ill, and the doctor said that he would not be able to be at the meeting. On the Friday we went to the big hall where lots of people came for the meeting. As we climbed out of the car who do you think stood there but the pastor who had been in hospital. I got out of the car and jumped in the air for joy – God had answered our prayers. The pastor was told by the doctors to go back to the hospital on Monday after the conference meetings. On Monday he was driven back to the hospital to be told that all his tests were clear. Praise God! The last time I saw that pastor, he whispered in my ear that I was needed there and shouldn't go home.

One Sunday meeting we attended was always held at 5:00 p.m. Around fifty people appeared from nearby villages and packed the meeting. Afterwards, a young evangelist asked if we would walk to the next village to pray for a Christian lady who was dying. I wondered how since daylight came at 6:00 a.m. and darkness fell at 6:00 p.m. The young men with us said that they would hold our hands as we walked there, and that's exactly what they did. It would have been great if I had brought a torch! We walked over tough terrain to the next village and when we arrived the Christians brought out their plastic chairs between the shacks for a service. During the meeting, all I was thinking about was the sick lady. We foreigners gave our testimonies, and all there sang and had a wonderful service. While we sat outside the huts, a very big fat spider around four inches and dark in colour was walking between us. One man said, "Barbara, there's a big poisonous spider". I lifted my legs into the air and kept them there until it had walked past us and into a bush. In the morning, as I awoke under my mosquito net, God very clearly told me to read about Jairus' daughter in Matthew 9:18. What stood out to me was how Jesus took the girl by the hand in Mark 5:41–42 and told her to get up, and at that moment life returned to her.

We were finally taken to the sick lady. She lived in a shack with a base-floor (not many had a floor). She was laying on a mattress and had a mosquito net over her. A couple from Ireland prayed for her, and then I bent down, lifted the net, and then lifted up her limp hand. I couldn't hear her breathing. I prayed for her to be well and up to doing her jobs, and then we walked back to the house. I couldn't get the lady out of my head but felt God had done something for her. The next morning, we arose and walked to the school for a 7:00 a.m. gathering and again I was thinking about the lady. The young Irishman asked me what story I was giving to the children that morning. I told him that I had brought some flannel graphs with me and would tell them the story of creation from Genesis. We met in a hut with more than twenty children in it aged four to fourteen. The flannel graphs and figures were about eight inches high and were surrounded with beautiful trees, flowers, animals and wonderful colours. The Irishman was a painter so after school he started painting the walls of the school sky blue, and then painted lots of vegetation on them. The vegetation was big leaves, trees and flowers, and then he painted a rainbow over the doorway. Each day he painted another wall. In the afternoons, some of the children came back to watch him paint. We other adults painted groups of white daisies with yellow middles and long green stalks on the walls. The school was transformed by the end of the week, and it was now bright and colourful. We found a board over which I put a painted black cloth to tell the story of creation, the story of animals, and the story of Adam and Eve using the flannels. The children's eyes sparkled as they watched and listened to the story of God creating the world.

We eventually moved on and were taken to a baby hospital

where you could smell the odours as you entered through the doorway. The building was four-sided with a courtyard in the middle. The matron's office was on the left, and the corridor walls were painted pale blue halfway along the corridor. As we walked into the wards, the walls were black and damp looking. Some mothers were holding their babies in the wards while others were waiting for their babies to arrive. A lot of women travelled a long way to have their babies in that hospital. After the mothers had their babies, they had to do their own washing. I remember that as I entered the hospital, I felt an awful feeling because I knew that something was wrong. Going into the ward, I got an awful feeling again as we moved around to the beds. A mother located in the back right-hand corner was crying. Our interpreter said the mother was telling us that her baby had died. I asked if I could give her a hug, and then hugged her a long, long time. How awful I felt it must have been for her to see all the other mothers with their babies. The word God gave me for her was that she would have another baby the next year and that all would be well for her.

One evening, I was asked to pray for a family where the lady was possessed and needed deliverance. Her home had lovely furniture, but you could feel something was wrong which we quickly identified. First, the family was given counsel, and then I was to pray for the lady (who was by now on the floor). I had a vision in which God showed me an animal stretched on the floor, lying there as if life had been taken out of it. God told me to command it to leave the house, which I did, and with that the door of the room slammed shut and I knew that it had left the house. The lady got up and sat on the settee looking like a different person. I remember saying to her that her countenance had changed – God had freed her. Her husband told me that he saw a huge difference in her, and then asked for us to pray for their sons to receive the Holy Spirit. After we prayed over them, we returned to the mission house to pack our bags for the long journey home.

On my last evening at the mission house, I was able to bless the pastors with some British money, which they could take to the bank and exchange. The next day a young Indian man drove us to the airport in Guwahati to begin our long journey back to England. It took two plane flights and two underground train rides to get home. All the travel in planes, trains and cars to, from, and in India were entirely worth it. What an experience it was seeing so many Indian adults and children finding Jesus. Seeing them find Jesus as their Saviour not only changed their lives but also mine. Praise God with us, for He kept us, and His kingdom was extended.

Chapter Eleven: Elaine Price
Wales, UK

To God be the Glory! Great Things He Has Done!
Great is the Lord, and highly to be praised; and His greatness is unsearchable. (Psalm 145:3 NASB)

When I was invited to go to India to minister, I immediately felt in my spirit that I should go. There were times during the trip when I found myself, and those who travelled with me, in some rather challenging situations! However, it all proved to be an exciting and amazing adventure.

Since the 1800's, Welsh missionaries have travelled to the Khasi Hills in Northeast India to evangelize the tribal people and plant churches. Now, I was invited to go to Shillong in the Khasi Hills to minister and meet these people. I asked my friend Gill Witton if she would accompany me and was very grateful that she agreed, believing that this was definitely God-ordained.

In 1841, missionaries Thomas and Annie Jones went to the Khasi Hills and built many Presbyterian churches. The Thomas Jones School of Mission and Evangelism that was built in Shillong in 2000 is testimony of the respect people still have for the Jones'.

Years later, following the Welsh Revival of 1904, Evan Robert's sister Mary and her husband Reverend Sydney Evans went to the Khasi Hills along with many other missionaries. The revival fire that they carried set rural churches all over the Khasi and Jaintia Hills ablaze in 1905 to 1906, which is recorded in history as the Khasi Hills Revival.

I was deeply touched on learning of the hardships that the Welsh people had endured in getting to India. It took them three months of travelling by boat and horseback. Some lost their lives before they even arrived there, and many lived and died there between 1841to1966.

When Gill and I went to Shillong, we were shown hospitals, schools, colleges and Welsh chapels that had been built there, and saw many plaques commemorating the Welsh people who had built the structures. People were hugely grateful to the missionaries who had given their lives over the years for them to receive the gospel. In 2006 thousands gathered in the village of Mairang to celebrate the anniversary of the 1906 revival. The celebration was organized by the Presbyterian church. God answered the cries of the people praying for revival and poured out His Spirit on them again in Mairang, and all over the Khasi and Jaintia Hills, which is exactly as it had happened before! The fire of God swept everywhere at once in a matter of months. Thousands were praying and worshipping God and were in deep repentance. Children and young people were at the forefront of it, which affected the schools in a big way. The people were fervently begging God to forgive them of their sins and deeply interceding for their unsaved families. Almost immediately, broken families and the unsaved were made whole.

Gill and I heard story after story of the amazing things that went on. However, the intensity of it had waned somewhat since then, but we saw plenty of evidence that God was still at work in the lives of people. The enemy had come in hard, and much spiritual warfare was still ongoing. People learnt of the gaps they felt that needed to be corrected, such as the need for more Bible teaching. We saw some new Bible colleges that had been built since then and others that were in the process of being built, and we visited one that was held in a converted garage. This, then, was the background of what we were entering into.

The first exciting adventure we had was travelling by helicopter from Tura to Shillong. If we were to drive, it would have taken us about nine or more hours on windy, bumpy roads. We heard that there was a possibility we could go by helicopter, but that there were no seats available. We really prayed there would be seats made available. God was merciful to us as that proved to be the case. We were very, very grateful to see God's hand at work.

The hospitality of the people was extraordinary and wherever we went a sumptuous meal was always served. We were very touched that a spritely man of ninety-two years insisted on taking us out to a very posh restaurant for a meal, and he insisted that we were to have anything on the menu that we fancied. Such was his gratitude to the Welsh people. We have many such precious memories.

During our time there, a house bound elderly man had heard from a pastor that we had a tallit (prayer shawl). He dearly wanted to see it and requested we pray for him under it. We were stuck in a traffic jam for about an hour getting there, but the look on his face when we arrived was worth it all. The presence of God was so powerful in that house. We also prayed for his beautiful daughter-in-law who was not able to conceive. A local taxi driver sat in the house to wait for us while we ministered. As we reached our next destination, he asked if we would pray for him because his wife could not conceive. How amazing! We are still waiting for a report.

One day, a youth pastor named JT took us to a local mixed school of some seventy to one hundred children aged between eight to fifteen years, all Khasis. They sat outside, smartly dressed in red uniforms and very well behaved. I spoke a little on Evan Roberts and how he had to leave school at nine years of age to work in the coal mine, and that he was in the chapel every night in prayer meetings. I then told them that he later became the man most associated with the Welsh Revival. I also took the opportunity to preach the gospel message, as I was told that there were many unsaved there although it was a Christian school. Gill gave a very anointed prayer and they started lining up to be prayed for. We must have prayed for nearly all of them, many falling in the Spirit. Many asked us to pray for their parents, and many tears were shed. The headmistress told us later that she was worried that many of the children were backsliding. She was very happy with our visit, believing it to be God's timing. We began to realize that many of the children were recommitting their lives to God. At one time a very thick cloud enveloped us, and the presence of God was so strong. All schoolwork was put on hold for around four and a half hours. We discovered that though it was a long meeting we were not even tired, but invigorated. The Holy Spirit was so powerful. When we left, a lot of smiling happy children waved us off.

Upon leaving, I was told I had three services lined up for the following Saturday and Sunday. The plan was that the morning meetings were for the youth, but I'm really glad to report that they chose to stay on for the whole day. The Sunday meeting was so powerful. I would say we were in revival, as the worship was amazing. The afternoon meeting was the main event. I shared on Ruth and Naomi, and the need for the church to love the Jews as Ruth loved Naomi. As revival was so close to people's hearts, I suggested there first needed to be a revival of love for God's people – Israel. I explained that God calls Israel the apple (or pupil) of His eye, which is the most tender part of His eye.

> I have great sorrow and unceasing grief in my heart.
> My heart's desire and my prayer to God for [Israel] is for their salvation. (Romans 9:2, 10:1 NASB)

Paul was echoing the heart of God in Romans 9 and 10. Gill and I encouraged the people to set their heart to echo the heart of God. Gill made a passionate altar plea for people to answer the challenge and go forward to make a commitment. We asked four men to hold the tallit and many, many people came away from the altar with tears streaming down their faces. I truly believe that a powerful spirit of intercession for the Jewish people was released. The queue for prayer never seemed to abate, with people queuing down the corridor. We later learnt that in the evening meeting Hindu Christians had joined the queue as did all the pastors. Gill and I were happy to be prayed for by them at the end. They in turn prayed for Wales to be ignited by the fire of God again. Amen, we agree. We were to hear those prayers many times actually, in every congregation we went to, as they have never stopped praying for Wales because of their gratitude towards the Welsh people. As I looked at congregation after congregation, I was seeing with my own eyes the fruit of seeds planted by the Welsh people so many years ago. What a privilege.

We had very encouraging feedback several days later from two youth pastors of different churches. They had already devoted a whole meeting to praying for Israel, using the prayer points that I had given. I had also left them photographs of men and women in the Israel Defence Force, to have a visual point of contact. One could see they were treasuring them. I gave one lady similar photographs and she said that she would hang them on the wall of her new Bible college. She said that God had put it on her heart many years ago to learn more about His chosen ones. She said that when we came, the burden increased so much she had started including teachings about Israel in her sermons. We had so much positive feedback it just thrills our hearts.

I'll finish with an unusual aspect of revival. We had been taken to a little country church to minister, and it was getting darker. When I looked outside, I was very surprised to see what I thought were people laid out in the Spirit outside the door. I thought this was very unusual, and then on closer inspection I could see that they were big dogs. I was told that ever since the revival had come the dogs would always come to the evening meetings and lie sprawled out outside the door. I was also told that a leopard came once and that beautiful, rare birds came and stayed in the church while meetings were going on. The birds also went to the homes of children who were touched with the revival. Is this a foretaste of Isaiah 11?

> The wolf also shall dwell with the lamb, The leopard shall lie down with the young goat, The calf and the young lion and the fatling together; And a little child shall lead them. The cow and the bear shall graze; Their young ones shall lie down together; And the lion shall eat straw like the ox. The nursing child shall play by the cobra's hole, And the weaned child shall put his hand in the viper's den. They shall not hurt nor destroy in all My holy mountain, For the earth shall be full of the knowledge of the Lord As the waters cover the sea. (Isaiah 11:6–9)

When I returned home, someone asked me what I came

back with. I didn't hesitate with my answer. It was, and is, the belief that God wants to move by His Spirit in Wales again. With that, I'm praying for revival for our nation again, and asking, "Will you join me?"

A Brief History of my Ancestor Reverend William Williams

My ancestor Reverend William Williams was a Welsh missionary to Meghalaya and Mizoram in Northeast India. In the June/July 1891 issue of Y Goleuad (Welsh Presbyterian Periodical Magazine), he published an appeal to open a mission station in the Mizo Hills in Northeast India. In June 1892, the Welsh General Assembly at Machynlleth, Wales decided to adopt the Mizo Hills as an extension of the Khasi Hills' Meghalaya mission field. However, before the decision was made, Reverend Williams died of typhoid on 21 April 1892, near Shillong City, but his work would have an everlasting impact on many.

It was from Mizoram that God's musical would be orchestrated. The once forbidden gate of South Manipur opened to an ambitious young man from Caernarvonshire, Mid Wales, who was not formerly trained or selected to be a missionary. That young man was none other than Watkin R. Roberts, a chemist who was born on 21 September 1886. Roberts was burdened so much for lost souls he dedicated his life to saving souls for the Lord in any capacity in which the Lord ordained him to serve. At one afternoon meeting of the Keswick Convention in 1908 before coming to Mizoram, he listened with rapt attention to Doctor Peter Fraser's passionate evangelistic plea for hundreds of tribes in Assam and Northeast India who were in utter darkness. They needed the gospel; they needed Jesus to save them from their heathen darkness.

The words inflamed Roberts enthusiastically. Placing himself at his Lord's command, in wishful imagination he began flying over mountains and oceans. Knowing not what his Lord had planned for him, Roberts accompanied Doctor Fraser and his wife (the first medical missionary to Mizoram) on 14 October 1908 to help them in their clinic. Both Roberts and Fraser attended the Castle Square Presbyterian Church of Wales, Caernarvon, Mid Wales. They left behind the conditions of ease, comparative luxury and the comfort of their homes in Wales.

A small gift of five pounds was sent to Watkin Roberts by his friend, Ms. Emily Davies who was, according to Roberts, a great prayer warrior. Roberts prayerfully considered how the money might be used to the best advantage for the furtherance of the gospel. Nothing is too small for God – with those five pounds Roberts was able to purchase enough bound booklets of the gospel of John in the Mizo language to present one to each village chief in Mizoram. Along with the presentation of the booklet was a letter explaining the way of salvation through Christ. It was suggested that the recipient read carefully John 3:16. They were also asked to acknowledge receipt of the booklet and to let Roberts know what was being done with the booklet.

By chance, one stranger, perhaps from the village of Senvon in Tipaimukh, Manipur, happened to be visiting the mission dispensary at Aizawl. On being told that missionary work was being done among the tribe, Roberts sent one copy of the Lushai dialect booklet through a stranger to the chief of Lenvon, named Kamkhawlun.

Knowing not the context and meaning of the booklet, Kamkhawlun sent back the booklet with an appeal written onto the leaf saying, "Sir, come yourself and tell us about this book and your God". Several months later, at an evening church meeting, D.E. Jones (the first Welsh missionary) announced a gospel of John booklet was returned from Manipur with a request for a missionary to come and explain the book. This arrested Robert's attention. He knew that it was the one that he had personally sent to Manipur and that the touching request was for the sender to visit the country personally. It was indeed a Macedonian call to go to a land and people who were still in spiritual darkness and bondage.

Roberts began looking for people who were familiar with the topography of the land between Mizoram and Manipur. Two men who were studying there volunteered to accompany Roberts on the aggressive and dangerous journey. Despite the perils and hardship involved, Roberts could see a rich harvest ahead for himself and his team. After a hazardous journey on foot for several days, the team arrived at Senvawn, Manipur on 5 February 1910. The Lord worked wonders.

Leaving aside their heathen practices, five people including the chief turned to the true and living God. The young converts went about telling the people of the unspeakable joy that was theirs. The good tidings soon swept across the mountains like a mighty tornado. Amazement and awe filled the hearts of all who heard it.

How could all this happen? It started with a humble but prayerful gift from a lady in Caernarfon. It was indeed an imperishable monumental work for the glory of the Lord. Roberts was simply an instrument through whom the lady spoke indirectly from her home in Wales to the hungry souls living thousands and thousands of miles away. Is it not wonderful? Paul planted; Apollos watered, and God gave the increase so that both he that planted, and he that watered are one.

The Northeast Manipur hill territory had already been illuminated with the light of the gospel. This was as a result of the tireless efforts of the Reverend William Pettigrew who had formerly worked for the Arthington Aborigines Mission. The mission was named after Robert Arthington, a millionaire from Leeds, who later joined the American Baptist Foreign Mission Society.

The darkness of centuries passed away and a new dawn of hope and love glowed brightly over the hills and mountains of Northeast India. The churches grew and flourished in the best tradition of the apostolic times of self-supporting, self-governing and self-propagating. This was the secret success of the missionary movement in this part of the world. The apostle Paul said that the gospel is the power of God unto which there is salvation for everyone that believes (Romans 1:16). It was not British imperialism or western civilization that changed the people, it was the power of the gospel of Christ that marvellously transformed the ignorant into enlightened ones. What a victory! The missionaries taught forgiveness, and to replace hatred with love and kindness for cruelty – attributes of the love of Christ. The missionaries devoted their entire lives, at tremendous personal sacrifice, to serve among the people. Some of the missionaries laid down their lives for the sake of the cross. It was the blood and testimony of those who died, and the dedicated services of those who are still alive who have united the distant hills of Northeast India with Wales. More importantly, it is the precious blood of Jesus Christ that made us one. We are all one in Christ.

Chapter Twelve: Keith Wilson
England, UK

My Life Changed

On 15 June 1974, I married into a Methodist family and moved to live and farm near the village of Bramley Moor in England. I attended the village church there with Monica my wife and her two boys from her first marriage. Over the years, I couldn't see any advantage of being a member of the church that had no answers to life's problems, in fact, I was becoming a worse person than I used to be. I would say then that if this is Christianity, I don't want it, although I did believe God created the world.

In 1985, whilst on holiday in Tenerife, Spain we heard a message of salvation from various preachers at South Tenerife Christian Fellowship (STCF). Then in Tenerife in 1993, Edward my son, his friend Charles and I were climbing in the mountains behind Playa de las Americas. Coming down the mountain, the boys wanted to find another way down other than the way we had gone up, which was not a proper path. I set off before them and was 100 feet below when they came running after me. They had dislodged a large bolder and I watched as it was coming towards me. I had nowhere to get out of its path and I knew I was going to be crushed to death. I wasn't afraid but had a sense of peace about me and joy in my heart. I dropped to the ground and waited. It went over me, and I survived without a scratch.

The boys came to me and said, "We thought you were a goner". I just laughed and joked with them the rest of the way down because I knew within my heart that I had met with the Lord on that mountain. That night I gave my life to Him, but it wasn't until later in my walk with the Lord that I realised what He was showing me on that mountain. I had to die to the world and be alive in Christ (Colossians 3:3; Galatians 2:20).

I had given my life to the Lord, but my life had not changed, in fact, it had gotten worse. My marriage relationship was becoming strained, and I made some bad decisions like losing money, and other things. In February 1996, I asked Pastor Tom Reston at STCF in Los Christianos to pray for me. From then on, my life began to change, and I started reading the word of God.

Missionary Call

In 1997 we returned to Tenerife and stepped into God's missionary plan over my life. At the Sunday morning meeting of STCF, my friend Mary brought her friend June Barron to give her testimony "From Witchcraft to Christ". After the meeting I invited Mary and June to lunch. That evening we went to a Spanish and English-speaking church with friends. The missions pastor was leading praise and worship, and each time he raised his arms I saw them glow fluorescently. June told me later that God was showing her (and evidently me) the anointing on him. After the meeting we went back to our friend's house where June spoke about the anointing on the missions pastor. Later that week I was baptised in the Holy Spirit. A few months later my wife Monica and I started a house group, and soon I was reading books on faith by Kenneth Hagin that taught me how to pray scriptures. At a training weekend that I attended in Sheffield, I met a lady who had a cancer that left her breathless when trying to walk only a few yards. During ministry time, God put us together and told me to cast out a demonic spirit from her. She agreed to let me pray for her, and I watched as the Lord healed her and she started running with ease. The Lord said to me, "Don't let that be a sign that you are right with me. I have not shown you this way of sanctification".

India, 1998–2001

My first mission trip was in November 1998 to India with June Barron as a member of her missionary team. During the trip, an evening meeting was held at Zawar Mines in Rajasthan and led by Bob, Linda and Duncan, all of whom were from the Isle of Man in the UK. Bob was asked to share with the church about how wrong it was for them to have their children's lives led by the stars when they had become believers. After Bob finished speaking, people lined up for prayer. I was interceding for the team when Duncan came up and told me to lay hands on the children. I was rather hesitant; however, a woman brought her daughter to me. I lifted my hand, put it on her head and upon doing so, she bent down and then shot back several feet and laid flat out. I was then swamped by mothers pushing their children forward for prayer. I couldn't believe my eyes.

In 1999, I once again joined June and her missionary team, this time in Shillong City in Northeast India. We were invited to Pastor D's church, where I was asked to give the Sunday afternoon and evening messages, though I had not preached in a church before. On Saturday night, I went before the Lord for a message. He gave me 2 Kings 23:1–20 and told me how to give it from a born-again believer's aspect. At the end of the meeting, the Lord prompted me to give an altar call. One elderly man came forward. Pastor D didn't recognise who he was, but turned to me and said, "Keith, this man is dumb (mute)". Pastor D laid his hands on him and commanded the mute spirit to leave. Immediately the man spoke and accepted Jesus Christ as his Saviour and walked out of the church praising God just like the account recorded in Mark 7.

In October 2001, I was travelling with June and a young evangelist named Miss Tialhmachhnani (Mimi) and the Holy Ghost Crusaders to Shillong, Meghalaya. On our journey, we stayed at a guest house run by a Muslim family. Before leaving the next morning, the owner of the guest house brought his sister to me for prayer. She had been suffering from severe stomach pains. I spoke over her what Jesus had done for her on the cross. I took authority over the spirits of fear and infirmity, commanded them to leave her, and then thanked the Lord that she was healed by the wounds and stripes that Jesus bore on the cross at Calvary. The Lord healed her instantly. She then brought her twelve-year-old daughter, who was mute to us for prayer. I asked her to open her mouth and it looked as if her tongue grew bigger. After we had finished praying, we coaxed her to say mummy and daddy. Praise the Lord, she said it!

Later that month, Mimi and her team were holding meetings in Mizo churches in Shillong City at the Thlarau Thianghlim Crusade. Mimi was preaching in one of the churches and the Lord was doing a lot of wonderful things. As some stepped inside the church, they fell to the floor. People were being set free and in doing so many were rededicating their lives to Christ. At the end of one of the meetings, two of the stewards brought a man to me for prayer who had a problem with his leg and a partially paralysed arm. As I prayed for him, the promises of the Lord and the work of Jesus on the cross came over him. The Lord healed him, and he danced and raised his hands in the air. Thank you, Lord! I asked the Lord, "Why don't we see things like this in the United Kingdom?" He replied, "I have done it all before, but what have you done with it?" The truth is, instead of keeping the world out of the church, we have brought the world into it (Proverbs 4:20–22).

Tenerife, 2003

In 2003, my wife and I were on our annual visit to Tenerife. One day, I was speaking at our friend's house group on divine healing. At the end of the meeting, a lady told us her story. She became a believer at an early age, but at the age of fourteen she had feelings and thoughts of wanting to have relationships with girls, rather than boys, which she knew was against the word of God. She spoke to her pastor about it, and he told her not to tell anyone, and that the Lord would take the thoughts away; however, the feelings remained. Eventually she got married and had children, but also had affairs with women, so consequently her marriage broke up. She went to Tenerife to start a new life and joined a church, but soon afterwards she got involved with another woman, which made her feel guilty and suicidal. I said to her, "Can I get you to believe that those thoughts and feelings don't belong to you as a new creation in Christ, but that they are from the devil?" She agreed and I then took authority over the demonic spirit that was affecting her, and later taught her how to overcome the thoughts and feelings. We left Tenerife later that week, but when we met up the following year, she came to us at church and told us she was so happy and had a male friend. Praise the Lord! He honours His word (John 8:36).

India, 2003–2008

It was in 2003 in Northeast India when I sponsored two schoolgirls through a ministry associated with June. My wife and I had already sponsored some children in the school, but as I was walking away from the school the Lord put on my heart that there were still some children who needed sponsoring, and He wanted me to do it. When I enquired, the teacher told me that there were two girls whose sponsorship was running out at the end of term – their names were Evangeline and Diaris. And so, we became sponsors of these two girls. On a return trip that I made in 2005, I was with the girls buying new glasses for Diaris when they both said that they wanted to accept Jesus as their Saviour. Two local pastors took the girls and another young man to a nearby village to be baptized in the river. Evangeline became a strong believer and helped me minister to the people (Matthew 28:19–20).

I am reminded of a couple stories of how blessed I was to witness Evangeline's spiritual growth. One such time was in 2005 when two local pastors asked Evangeline and me to go to the hospital with them to pray over a young teenager from their church who had been taken to hospital very ill. He was suffering from tuberculosis, but his parents couldn't afford to keep buying the medicine he needed. He hadn't been to church recently, so no one knew the circumstances of the family. We prayed for the boy, believing for a miraculous recovery, but he passed away that night, and we had to pick up the body the next morning. When they placed the body in the community ambulance, Pastor J told me to pray over it. We were all hoping that God would raise him from the dead, but it wasn't to be. Evangeline's faith was not hindered but strengthened, as at the funeral during prayer she wanted to be baptised in the Holy Spirit, and the Lord blessed her with tongues (1 Corinthians 14:2). The second time was in 2006 when Evangeline, her cousin Onita and I went to visit someone whose son had depression, and a very unkempt appearance. As we were praying for him, and a spirit came upon him that caused him to act like a wild animal. As I laid my hand on him, he was reacting violently, so we had to hold him down. We took authority over the demonic spirit, but nothing left him. I asked who the spirit was, and it answered Legion. I was led by the Spirit of God to have him to go through a prayer of salvation, and then to baptise him in the Holy Spirit. After more than an hour of the demons trying to stop him from speaking, we got him through the prayer and speaking in tongues. He repented of the Khasis rituals he had learnt as a child, and then finally the demons left him after a two-hour battle. Evangeline and Onita, only young believers, were brave and courageous as they worked with me as though they were mature believers. Praise the Lord for His Spirit working through us (Ephesians 3:20–21).

In 2008, I was in Aizawl, Mizoram in Northeast India. A man in Nazareth Hospital had sent a request to Mimi at Faith Ministries to visit him after having an unsuccessful surgery for cancer of the oesophagus, from which he was dying. As I was staying with Mimi, she asked if I would like to visit him. I was taken by a young believer on a motor bike to a person who would interpret for me. The man was in a single room, he was very weak and had a drip in his vein. He said that he was not afraid to die but did not know what happened after death. I said that I could tell him according to the word of God and His promises. He listened to me, and then I asked him and his wife if they would like to receive Jesus as their Saviour and have the promises that went with it. They said yes, and I took them through a prayer of salvation, but the man was too exhausted to do anymore. I asked his wife if she would go through prayers of repentance on behalf of both of them, and prayers of dedication to Jesus along with repentance, forgiveness and breaking the curse of illness. Before leaving I prayed for his healing, proclaiming the work of Jesus on the cross, thanking the Father for the blood of Jesus, and asking that all curses be broken, and all sins forgiven in Jesus' name. I said that I would visit again before leaving Mizoram. Five days later I again visited him. He was sitting up in bed, still on a drip, but full of life! He told me that the night after my visit he had a vision of being in heaven. Now he knows that there is a God and when people visit him, he tells them that there is a God in heaven. Praise the Lord! We give Him all the glory (Psalm 103:2; Matt. 8:17).

Give Thanks to the Lord

I thank God for all the strong believers He has brought into my life and for teaching me so many things. Since the day I accepted Jesus as my Lord and Saviour in 1993 at the age of forty-eight, I have seen the Lord do so many wonderful things in India with June's mission trips and elsewhere. The stories I've shared here are but a few of the ways the Lord has used me and those around me and intertwined my life with others to touch His beloved children.

I give all the glory to my Lord.

Chapter Thirteen: Gill Witton
Wales, UK

I had been to India a few times but one particular year I was invited by my friend Elaine Price to accompany her on a trip there. Our journey would take us to Northeast India where we would minister to the people in Shillong, which is in Meghalaya.

Ministry began the evening of our arrival. The meeting was held in the home of a lady that both Elaine and I had met during a previous trip to India. We had the honour of praying for several people during the visit before we shifted to the home of a friend for a meal and prayer. Praise God, many received healing each place the Lord took us that evening.

The following day was the Sabbath day, a day recognized as being all about quality family time, husbands blessing their wives and children, and wives blessing their husbands. This day brought us to a police fellowship held in a home. Since it was the Sabbath day, Elaine gave a message about the Sabbath. As God would have it, and without our knowledge, the lady of the house who, despite much secular counselling, had many unresolved family problems. This night became one of divine counselling for the lady as she sat under the Sabbath teaching about family on a day set aside by the Lord in ages past.

On Sunday, a young man named JT took us to his church for multiple services that they held. We listened to an anointed message about the Passover, and then were blessed to pray for a few people. After a quick break for lunch, the people gathered in the church once again to hear a message about the Prodigal Son. It was a lovely meeting as the Spirit moved amongst the people and it was especially lovely seeing a man delivered and filled with the gift of the Holy Spirit.

Monday was another eventful day. The morning started with a severe thunderstorm that caused our bedroom to flood due to a breakage in the drainage system in the en-suite shower. Happily, a group of boys soon came and sorted out the problem before we left to visit a village Presbyterian church with local friends Ricky and Audrey. Upon arriving we had the customary warm Indian welcome and a time of tea. When the morning church bells rang, the people filled the church to receive the message "The King is Coming". Once again, we were blessed to pray for the people after the service, and then had a lovely lunch at the pastor's house. It was soon time to get back into the car and continue on to the next location. The drive to the next church took several hours and was through beautiful countryside with beautiful views. We stopped to have tea along the way at a cafe that had a beautiful view of a mountain. As we took in its beauty, a cloud-like smoke came down on the mountain, and then lifted to reveal a golden light on top of the mountain before quickly turning red. It was absolutely amazing. When we arrived in the next village at the Presbyterian Church where we were to speak, we first had an evening meal at a friend's house before attending the service. We were full of expectancy during the service, as Elaine gave a message on the book of Esther. At the end of the message, there was a call to come forward for prayer and to make a commitment like that of Esther and Mordecai. There were more than 250 people present at the service, and many came forward, including a Hindu man

Chapter Thirteen: Gill Witton

who came forward for prayer. Apparently, the Hindu man's wife was a Christian, but he wouldn't receive Jesus as his Lord until that moment in the service. News of him receiving Jesus as his Lord later caused a real stir in the community and quickly spread across the region. His coming forward paved a way, as people began asking where we are going next so they could hear more.

The following morning, we had to get up early to travel to Pastor M's church, youth hostel and school in Shillong City for a week of ministry mixed with fellowship. During the daytime we taught the students and in the evening we joined in their church service.

At our first daytime meeting with the students, we taught about Elisha receiving a double portion of Elijah's anointing, and afterwards we prayed for all those present to receive a double portion. Some of the students had a seer anointing and some a prophetic anointing. After we prayed over them, the students went out into the town evangelizing. The next day, we taught about the Prodigal Son and his jealous brother after which we prayed over them and encouraged them to confess and repent to God privately of their sins. As we prepared to teach the following day about the Feast of Passover, Pastor M told us not to hold anything back as his student had no understanding about Passover and were very excited to learn. After the Passover teaching, one young female student told me that her friend had phoned earlier to say that she should keep the Passover, though she had no understanding of it at the time.

One afternoon, we were to give two messages. Elaine started the meeting with the hymn that is often said to be the love song of the Welsh Revival called "Dyma Garied". We all sang along in the Holy Spirit. Everyone came forward, many crying, and knelt at the altar before God. The pastor prayed for them as they were on their faces before God, and many let go of their unforgiveness. One young girl began prophesying in her heavenly language and Pastor M's wife interpreted, which led to receiving further prayer from Elaine, and then prayer for the revival fire of God to fall. Pastor M's wife shared a vision from the Lord of a very large, beautiful house, but that it then was burnt up by a fire. The house was good on the outside but needed cleaned up inside. During the meeting people who didn't speak in tongues began singing in tongues. As the meeting finished everyone passed under the Holy Spirit.

Hearts were changing, and now the Feast of the Pentecost was upon us and so was a teaching about it. Students were busy taking notes during the teaching, after which they all held hands and asked to be baptised in the Holy Spirit and the fire of God. Elaine and I prayed for them to receive the gift of speaking in tongues. Some of them were speaking in tongues with the fire of God coming out. They were all falling in the Spirit, and then a chorus of Hebrew songs broke out.

Later, Elaine gave a message on the book of Ruth that was greatly received with lots of prayer for Israel. Students knelt down and prayed over the Israeli flag and a picture of Israel Defence Forces. A holocaust teaching was then given and a video on aliyah shown. Elaine then shared the story of Esther and Mordecai, and they all responded to the call of God. Many people said that they were so excited because they had never heard such a teaching. Toward the end of the meeting, Pastor M prayed a lovely prayer and shared that he felt his heart was being touched and asked for our forgiveness for not understanding. Pastor M's wife was lovely and prayed for both of them.

These are just a few stories amongst the many that I could share of how God moved during our time in India. We were blessed with the opportunity to pray for many people (young and old) and spend countless hours in ministry and fellowship with local pastors.

To God be the glory!

Photographs

Ashley Treacy transcribing testimonies

Premdan Majhi in a tea garden in India

Barbara Pollard (left) and June Barron at the conference in the Isle of Man

Photographs

Gladys Coutino with a rescued child at the orphanage in Northeast India

Gladys Coutino at a medical camp in Northeast India

Richard John Perry ministering in India

Malcolm Alcock teaching brick making in Northeast India

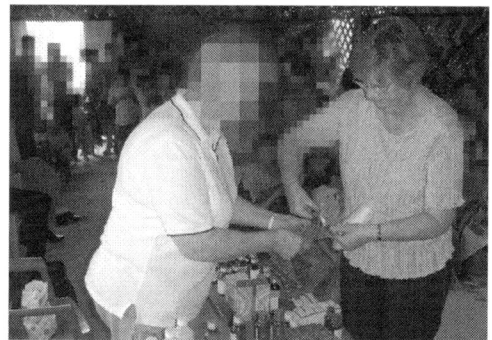

Marina Adams at a medical camp in Northeast India

Marina and Tommy Adams rescuing a baby in India

Photographs

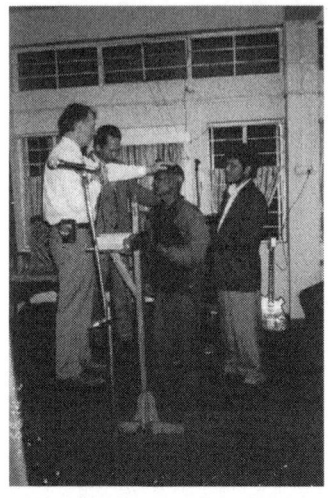

Keith Wilson praying for a sick man in Northeast India

Deborah Gaffney working with BFP food distribution in Israel

Keith Wilson ministering in Northeast India

Printed in Great Britain
by Amazon